Swallowtail Calling

Swallowtail Calling

A naturalist dreams of Grand Manan Island

Wendy Dathan

Shoreline

Front cover photograph by Katie Seiden
Back cover sketch by Nan Phillips
Graphic design by Sarah Robinson

Shoreline
23 Ste-Anne, Ste-Anne-de-Bellevue, QC H9X 1L1
514.457.5733 shoreline@videotron.ca
www.shorelinepress.ca

Dépôt légal: Library and Archives Canada
and Bibliothèque et Archives nationales du Québec

Printed in Canada by Transcontinental Metrolitho

Library and Archives Canada Cataloguing in Publication

Dathan, Wendy, 1934-
Swallowtail calling : a naturalist dreams of
Grand Manan Island / Wendy Dathan.
ISBN 978-1-896754-76-5
1. Dathan, Wendy, 1934- -Homes and haunts--New Brunswick--Grand Manan Island. 2. Naturalists--Canada--Biography. 3. Grand Manan Island (N.B.)--Biography.
I. Title.
QH31.D38A3 2009 508.092 C2009-902479-9

Daisies
are the colour of my island,
    for when I come
    to beach my heart
    on a herring shore,
    morning is always June.

Dedicated

to my friends from here and away
who have given me so many happy memories,

to my family who support me with such love
and gives me so much joy,

and to Tim who gave me my island home.

Contents

Adapted from map from Grand Manan Tourism Association.

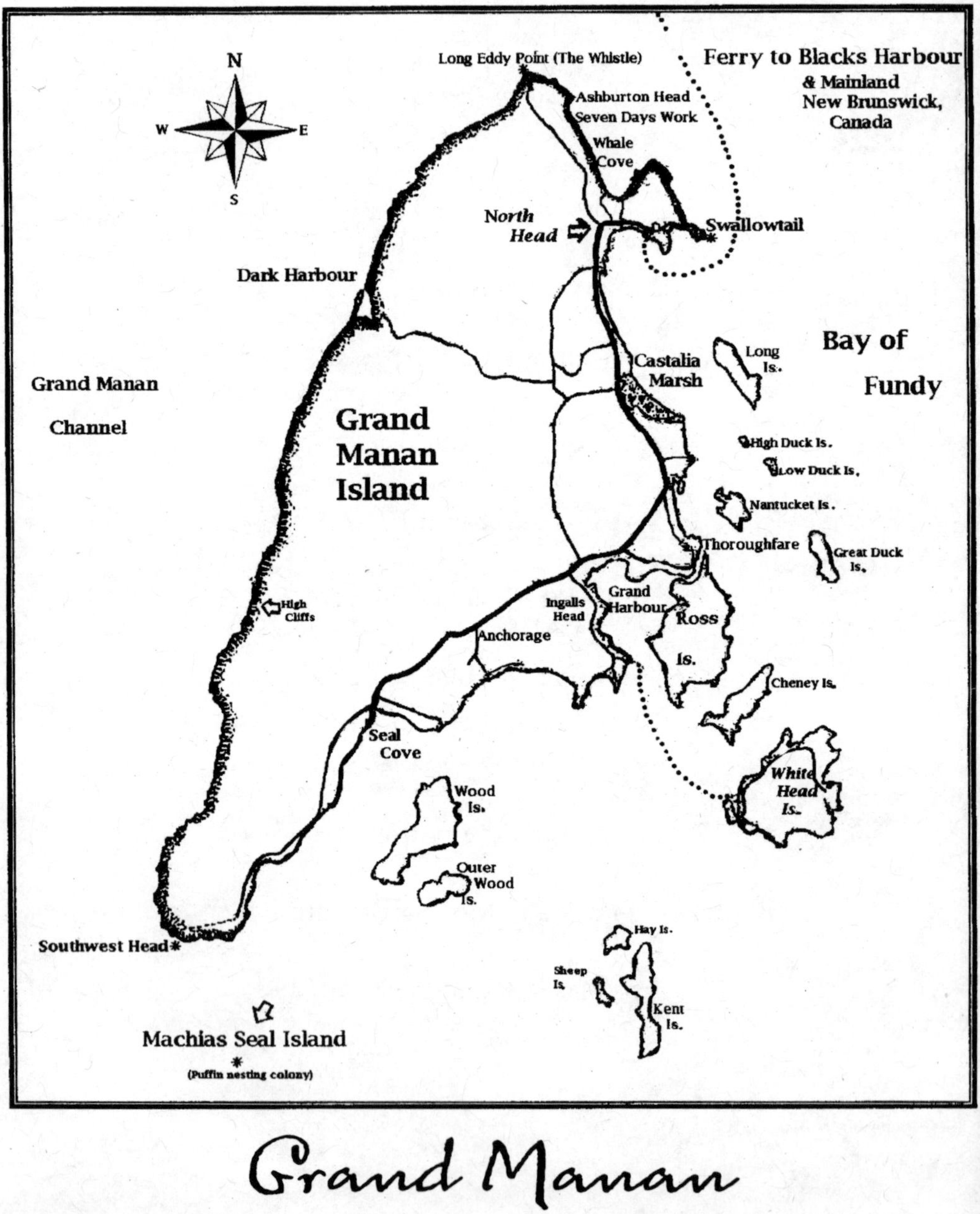

Grand Manan

"Going Home"

It is hard to remember a time when I had never seen Grand Manan Island, had never even found it on a map. Of course, when I looked it up, it was easy. Someone once described it as the dot at the end of the question mark formed by the line of the international border between the province of New Brunswick, Canada, and the state of Maine, U.S.A. It is a triangular dot at the mouth of the Bay of Fundy, that bay with the enormous tides, and there it is, a little island with a long base of basalt cliffs to the westward and an apex of low fishing settlements on the sides to the east and the south.

Although for more than a century the 'Queen of the Fundy Isles' was a cherished summer destination for artists, photographers, writers, hikers, naturalists, birders, botanists, whale watchers, and that special kind of visitor or seasonal resident who really wants to get away from it all, most of these people wanted to keep their refuge a secret. It became a cachet among naturalists as to who could be included in this special find of an unspoiled place to visit, rich in birds and flowers and lovely scenery, not to mention a place that was safe to wander and had friendly people to talk to – the chosen few were careful about who should know about their hideaway so the 'wrong kind of people' did not go there and spoil it. So it was not until I was initiated into the world of natural history that I began to hear more of the island and its attractions.

I do remember, however, the first time I heard the name 'Grand Manan'. I had been sent to a boarding school in post-war England, and our classroom, bright and airy in summer, perishing cold in winter, contained about twelve of us girls, all identically clad in navy blue uniforms. We were seated in neat rows in front of our teacher and were dutifully writing down dictated history notes crammed with royal lineages, wars and treaties. Apparently, islands were prime targets for exchanging ownership in treaty making. I have forgotten which war had just ended, but France had been the loser when she was forced to give up Grand Manan in exchange for some other island, possibly St. Pierre and Miquelon, to which she has hung grimly ever since. The Brits, as victorious winners (and in those history notes England was always the winner or else she 'stood alone' in the face of all evil), were very pleased to acquire a seven-by-eleven-mile dot on the globe that would provide a mooring for their warships if needed to secure the lands to the east, north and west of that deep-water Fundy gash into the Atlantic coastal interior.

Fortunately, the island was never needed as a site for sea battles, but there the name sat in the cobwebbed attic of my brain, unwanted and discarded, of no particular importance, except that like so many useless facts in my lifetime it had been implanted somewhere inside, and the next time I heard it was almost thirty years later on the opposite side of the Atlantic, close to the Arctic Circle, on Baffin Island on the top of the world.

My life now revolved around another island, this time the island of Montreal, Quebec. A group of naturalists and photographers from the newly formed Catherine Traill Naturalists Club in Ste. Anne de Bellevue had gone up to assist Dr. Dorothy Swales of Macdonald College with her Arctic botanical collecting in what was then Frobisher Bay and is now Iqaluit. There were six of us in all and we had a wonderful time exploring the tundra and the town that Prince

Philip had once christened a dump. Why clean it up, we all vaguely wondered, when the debris was cleansed in the wind and would all too soon be covered again with snow? We loved the open contours of the treeawfuls land, the colours of sea and rock and sky, the Inuit figures that looked like carvings of themselves as they went about their business, the nesting tundra birds, and the tiny wildflowers and miniature willows that we photographed and gathered as Dr. Swales pressed and preserved them. And we loved the sunsets, glorious in that brief late hour when the Arctic summer sun shy-kissed the horizon before coming back up beaming to embrace another nearly endless day.

Photographer Doris Mowry was with us on this trip. While we all admired the wondrous evening sky, she sniffed. "Not as good as Grand Manan," she would say. It seemed nothing was as good as Grand Manan. Grand Manan had not only the best sunsets but the best birds, the best wildflowers, the best beaches, the best scenery, the best everything.

We learned that Dr. Swales had been to Grand Manan in the 1960s, staying as all naturalists did at the time at Gerald L'Aventure's Anchorage Inn. Because she had no car, she spent most of her week collecting plants around what is now Anchorage Park. There was a group of birders also staying at the inn, and one evening the leader said, "Dr. Swales, I know a great deal about birds but very little about wildflowers. Would you feel like showing us some this evening?" A born teacher, she was only too happy to share her knowledge and love of the flora. When the dining area had been cleared after supper, she spread her plant collection for display, which is how she came to teach Roger Tory Peterson, the man who was to become so famous in birding circles all around the world, about the flowers of Grand Manan.

With all this talk, it was not surprising that a fellow northern traveller, Joan Rowe, and I decided while we were on Baffin Island that one day we would go to Grand Manan and see it for ourselves, but first, we had to say good-bye to Dr. Swales in Frobisher Bay. White-haired and vigorous in her mid-seventies, warm and fun-loving and totally dedicated to her scientific mission, she was a commanding figure as she strode about the tundra directing her unofficial subordinates and purposefully doing her bit to decimate the land of its rarest plant species. Part of her study included examining plant pollinators, for which purpose she carried a butterfly net, a piece of equipment that had arrived in separate parts but when assembled would no longer collapse and could not fit back into her suitcase. When she left us at the end of five days, it was raining in torrents. We accompanied her to the airport where she sat holding up her butterfly net with her usual innate dignity while curious Inuit giggled and laughed at this peculiar sight. She left us for Resolute in the High Arctic where she arrived in a snowstorm and disembarked still carrying the net. "Oh, my, Dr. Swales," said the smiling man who met her, "I don't think you'll find many butterflies here!"

Before the rest of us returned to Montreal, two of us made one last excursion to the graveyard, the place we had visited first, and collected a small Arctic garden to take home. Among the profusion of miniature plants we gathered in that desolate place, out on the beach we found a wide, flat circle of blue-green leaves and stems crowned with pink buds and blue flowers, the amphi-North-Atlantic Sea Mertensia, which

Joan and I would next find on the Anchorage Beach on Grand Manan.

It would be a year or two before we had a chance to make our first trip to the island, and when we did it would again be with the help of the naturalists club. I seem to count my years in decades, each one distinct from the others, and for me the decade that ushered in my fortieth year in the nineteen seventies was one of two important influences, Macdonald College and the Catherine Traill Naturalists Club.

I blame it all on India and wild food guru Euell Gibbons. I went to India in 1968 with my husband, who was there on business, and I came home devastated by the need that I had seen everywhere. I felt I had to do something, anything, to alleviate my sense of helplessness. I joined the Unitarian Service Committee to pack clothes to be sent out where needed, and we made packages to send off for babies in the refugee tent camps on the Gaza Strip, and quilts made of pockets that we sewed together to give someone warmth out there in the desperate world. I was horribly aware of North American lavish abundance and grieved at the terrible waste. People piled food on their plates, only to have much of it thrown away.

Not long afterwards, I picked up a book called *Stalking the Wild Asparagus*, and discovered that all around us was another kind of waste, edible wildflowers and wild fruits and weeds that went unused and neglected, and since I didn't know one plant from another, before long I gravitated to the botany part of the college where I met Dr. Swales and her assistant, Elizabeth Parnis, in the McGill Herbarium. Elizabeth had started the Catherine Traill Naturalists Club, and I was invited to the founding meeting, which opened up for me a whole new world. We went gathering wild foods together and planned a wild food dinner for the club and I took botany courses and assisted Elizabeth in an evening course in 'Edible Wild Plants'.

As part of that decade of naturalist exploration under the enthusiastic leadership of Chairman George McKiel, in 1978 the club organized a week at the Huntsman Marine Laboratory in St. Andrews, where we had a wonderful time playing at being marine biologists with leader Mike Butler. When it was over, a smaller number of 'Cat Nats' set off for Grand Manan in a convoy of cars. We drove to Blacks Harbour, that then dour one-company town soul-owned by Connors Brothers sardine empire, and lined up for the ferry at the end of the road. The black boat, the *Grand Manan IV*, was the main ferry in those days, with the smaller *Lady Manan* (not too affectionately known as 'The Car Wash' for her open deck and habit of rolling with the sea-splashing waves) acting as alternate transport in summer. We had timed our arrival for the larger vessel, and in due course our cars were crammed into the hold like appropriate Connors sardines.

Above deck, unlike the home-headed islanders who were soon sitting warmly and comfortably inside, like all tourists we headed for the wind and cold outside. Most of our group gathered at the rails to scan the horizon for marine birds and possible whales, but I had something else I wanted to do, something I wanted to do alone. I love the sea. I love the smell of seaweed and the sound of waves swelling and crashing on the shore. I love the taste of salt and the wind that sets me free. Above all, I love to stand at the very front of a moving boat in the same way I once stood at the bow of an ocean-going freighter heading for England one November, taking a turn at the watch in dense fog or just being there when nine porpoises appeared, so close I felt I could reach down and touch them as they leapt and swam beside us.

On the ferry, the crew had not yet put up a barrier across the area at the front, so I could stand right in the angle of the prow, and I stood there in what I can only describe as an aura of intense joy, breathing the fresh salt of the sea, hearing the noise of the engines aft and feeling her power as she dipped and rose over the water, ploughing her way southwards through the furrows of waves, out past the floating gulls and arcing porpoises, out to a faraway mound on the horizon shaped like a west-facing whale. Since this was my first time on these waters, I did not know that the imagined tail would turn out to be Swallowtail and the head the high northwest cliffs with a winking Whistle Lighthouse eye, but the dark shape ahead, growing ever larger as we neared it, seemed to promise a place where anything exciting could happen.

I don't remember how far out we were before something very strange happened to me, unlike anything I had ever experienced before. Suddenly, without warning, a voice in my head said, "I am going home." Going home! This was ridiculous! I had a family and a home in Montreal and I hadn't even seen the place yet! Where on earth did that come from? Yet there it was, this weird and unexpected sort of prophesy, and it left me feeling rather peculiar, wondering what kind of magic this island ahead of us held.

Slowly we drew closer to the island, past the Ashburton Head of so many shipwrecks, past the layered geological formation known as Seven Days Work, past Whale Cove, once the harbour of the warships in the British Navy, round the headland of Swallowtail with the last-built lighthouse in New Brunswick before Canada's Confederation, round the kidney-shaped herring weirs of which 'Corabelle' was the most famous, past pebbled Pettes Cove and the rounded towers of Irving Oil as the ferry gave her arriving toot and moved up to the wharf at North Head.

One should always write down first impressions, but of course I didn't, yet it is hard to escape a recurrent feeling that the beautiful thing about the harbour in North Head was and is still, although it may not be for much longer, the lack of yachts. There are beautiful harbours with yachts all over the world, full of those graceful playthings with elegant masts and sails, picturesque and wonderful, raising visions of fragility challenging the sea, but the beauty of North Head is their absence, which is rare and getting rarer in a fantasy world. The only boats we saw as we pulled into the wharf were working boats, dories, and lobster boats, weir pumpers, carriers and seiners, honest and sturdy and real, and instantly we knew why this place was special. It was like truth: it was new and different but it had no pretensions and it would not let us down.

There is a sort of disorderly tidiness about North Head, with its haphazard distribution of land space. Around the harbour we could see the neat white houses, each one differing from its neighbour, tacking down the road in anything but even lines. Above and to the west was a low ridge of upland, and going up the lane from the red-bricked post office, looking down on the boats below, was a large sprawling wooden building that had once been part of an old Sea Captain's house, the imposing-looking Marathon Hotel with its 'Widow's Walk' tower built to scan the sea for a hoped-for boat arrival. We had not come as a group intending to stay together so none of us would be staying at the hotel, at least not for the moment. Once the ferry had docked and opened its jaws to disgorge all the cars, we would be scattering all over the island to separate accommodations and we would meet again in a group only to go out to see the puffins at Machias Seal Island and for the special Saturday gourmet dinner at the Compass Rose.

One of our naturalist members had been to the island before. When Frank Chadillon let me in on the secret of his special hideaway, Joan and I booked a cabin in the same place. It was halfway down the one main road that ran from North Head to Seal Cove to the south, so driving southwards gave us a chance to see wonderful glimpses of outer islands, the wide expanse of Castalia saltmarsh, the picuresque Woodwards Cove harbour with its spectacular smoked herring sheds, and what seemed to be the centre of commerce at Grand Harbour with the bank and grocery-cum-hardware store, a miniature post office, a gift shop, the museum and elementary and high schools. At the corner by the stone Anglican church that was the oldest church on the island, we turned east towards Ingalls Head and were warmly welcomed by Jenny and Eldred Wilson at their assorted group of holiday accommodations, a delightfully eclectic assortment of housing that consisted of one trailer, one log cabin, one converted garage, and three tiny cabins from the old Anchorage Inn that Eldred had bought when the L'Aventures closed it down.

The other two members of our naturalist party, Frank and a nice artist called Ruth whom he was squiring around that year because, as he said, she didn't have much money and his regular companion was travelling in Europe, disappeared into the cabin by the shore. We had cabin #3, and were happy to see that it was clean and had all the essentials, and by morning we could settle down to serious naturalist business as we explored the island for the very first time.

We had a glorious week. We botanized, we birded, we hiked, we collected beach pebbles and shells and driftwood, we picnicked looking out over the sea. We climbed down the steps to Swallowtail Lighthouse, where my extension camera lens fell down several steps before luckily landing safely without breaking, and we looked down on the herring weirs below and watched the ferry rounding the point. On the beach at the Anchorage we found the wheel of Sea Mertensia that reminded us of the one we had seen on Baffin Island. We went to the Museum where Curator Elmer Wilcox told us where to find wild orchids in the wet bog at Ingalls Head, beautiful little Dragon's Mouth *Arethusas* and Grass Pink *Calopogons* no higher than the span of our hands. We took photographs of the harbour and the old fish factory at Ingalls Head, where the gulls lined up on the roof or rose in unison to meet an incoming fishing boat. We went to Seal Cove, redolent with the smell of smoking herring as we came down the hill, to the smoke houses where Dewey Joy showed us how it all worked, from the driftwood fires that he tended on the mud floor to the rows of strung fish turning golden up in the rafters above. We tasted tough dried pieces of that famous red seaweed known as dulse, that had to be dried in the sun for four hours before it could be billed as 'Fresh Dark Harbour Dulse – the best dulse in the world', and went out to see the dulse-gathering activity on the bar at Dark Harbour and met the 'Mayor' sitting on an old dentist's chair. We went into Eileen Somer's home shop and bought hobo bags decorated with a liquid-embroidered map of Grand Manan and loon piggybanks made of canvas covered in synthetic wool. We had ice cream at

Harbour Gifts, fish and chips at Fundy House, and we would have had 'Mrs. Murphy's chowder' at Liz Jennaway-Murphy's Grand Harbour Inn opposite St. Paul's church if we had not already booked to join the group at the Compass Rose.

Although we often ran into each other in smaller units, we did not meet as a group until the day that we all gathered on the dock at Seal Cove to go out with Preston Wilcox in his *Senorita* to see the puffins on Machias Seal Island. Seal Cove, at the southern end of the island, was undoubtedly the prettiest village we had seen. Even without the interesting area with the smokehouses, one had only to start down the hill to see the attractive well-built houses and striking twin churches to see that this was a community built on pride. Of course we heard the story from a local that someone had walked past the rival churches one Sunday and from the first church had heard the congregation singing "Will there be stars in our heaven?" and from the other "No, no, not one," but we were to learn that Grand Mananers loved these tongue-in-cheek side-swipes at each other as it was all good for a laugh.

With Preston at the wheel, we set off on a wondrous trip out past the southern end of the island, seeing the glacial erratic boulders for which the Lower and Upper 'Flock of Sheep' trails are named, past the high basalt cliffs, and out towards the low coast of Maine that marked the horizon way off in the distance, heading halfway out to a dot in the ocean swarming with overhead Arctic terns. And of course we fell head over heels in love with the puffins, those adorable clowns of the sea with their oversize beaks and shrewd little eyes and comic feet. By the time we arrived back at Seal Cove, we were a happy satisfied group, sated with birds and sun, salt and sea.

The special gourmet dinner at the Compass Rose, owned then by Linda L'Aventure and Cecilia Bowden, was held on our last Saturday, and consisted of several courses, each more delicious than the last. The old dining room off the front hall was quite tiny and was crammed with small tables, seemingly only inches apart. Somehow, we and several others were all fitted snugly inside. Ralph Hoskins and I were placed at a table by the front door, sharing it with strangers from Ottawa, Betty and Lloyd McDermot, who were staying at the 'Cliff by the Sea' cottages in Harrington Cove. There was a tall older man sitting at the next table who turned out to be Gerald L'Aventure. As he had done so often in the past at the Anchorage Inn where time had been measured in bells, every so often he would get up from his seat and ring a heavy ship's bell. Poor Ralph had his back to the corner and was completely unprepared for the sudden ear-startling sound. He nearly jumped out of his seat the first time it happened, so after that we tried to warn him before the bell was pealed.

While on Grand Manan on holiday, it was mandatory for tourists located down island, unlike those at the north end who went to the Whistle, to go down to Southwest Head to see the sunset. All the 'Cliff by the Sea' people went down regularly with Maude Hunter, always hoping it would be a good one. Sometimes it seemed very promising, but then on the drive down the sky would suddenly pale and grow timid and there would be an air of disappointment in the little throng of people standing on the cliffs watching it just sort of fade away. When it was good, it was magnificent, with sky and sea on fire, framed by the drama of the dark rocks below.

We would stand on the rim of the high western cliffs, formed of perpendicular columns of basalt rising abruptly out of the sea, remembering that this was once the site of a dramatic rescue of a fisherman stranded halfway down in a storm, and look out towards the coast of Maine where the only signs that the world was inhabited were the U.S. Navy towers at Cutler and the winking light halfway out in the ocean that was the Canadian Coastguard lighthouse on tiny Machias Seal Island. We would stand in silence as the great fiery orb of sun slowly became a half circle and then slipped below the darkening coastline in a final burst of sunset flames. When it was over, we could drive home in the dark with our heads full of afterglow satisfaction that another good day had ended well.

Joan and I went once to Southwest Head to see a good sunset, but on our usual evenings after supper we went walking down Ingalls Head road with our friends from the other cabin. Frank was a tall man, well over six foot in height, and he was blond and strikingly good looking. He always wore a bright red hat so he stood out like a scarlet-topped telephone pole on an empty highway. As each passing occupant of bike, car or truck waved or honked in our direction, Frank smiled and returned the wave. "They always recognize me when I come back," he beamed, as if this was quite extraordinary.

All during our week on the island, Frank went for long hikes alone while Ruth painted gentle watercolours and Joan and I went off on our naturalist adventures. Only once we went partway with him when he invited us to see a special plant he had found. I think I remember that it was a sundew in bloom but I can't be sure. I am sure that we found the going difficult, trying to keep up with him as he loped along, stopping to catch our puffing breaths, and watched with relief as he continued on down his marathon trail. So it came as a huge shock to us a few months later when we learned in Montreal that he had gone up to the Laurentians on another hiking holiday when he had suddenly collapsed and died of lung cancer. He had known all along and not mentioned it and we certainly never suspected it.

Our long-anticipated holiday on Grand Manan was ending. At that time, there was no way to book the ferry for the outward journey, so the last thing to do before leaving the island was to put the car in line at North Head. We envied the islanders who could put a temporary substitute vehicle to hold their place until ready to leave the next morning. Since we had a long drive ahead to get back home, Joan and I decided to spend the last night at the Marathon Hotel where we could leave our car in the line-up and just walk up the hill. We were given a huge, old-fashioned room with two enormous comfortable beds, and we slept like dormice after an evening in the drawing room where proprietress Fern Leslie played gracious hostess beside the grand piano. It seemed the perfect ending the next morning, to walk down the hill to the car with the smell of salt and boat in the harbour, to drive aboard the ferry and go round Swallowtail in the blessing of eastern sun.

"I will be back," I told the mystery voice in my head as the ferry pointed her prow northwards. "I'm going back to my other island home for now, but I will be back. Soon."

Naturalist Invasion

The Cat Nats went to St. Andrews again in 1979, but I was in England and had to miss that second happy week at the Huntsman. When they did it again in 1980, I was more than ready, and at the end of the week another group of us headed for Blacks Harbour and the ferry to Grand Manan.

So once again the island swarmed with Montreal naturalists, those funny people with Tilley hats and cameras and field glasses, those strange 'from-away' people who were always gazing off in the distance or crawling around on their hands and knees, to the great amusement of the islanders, although they were perhaps not so much of a nuisance as some of the regular tourists. Grand Mananers are innately polite and friendly and one of the island's most precious attractions is that, like the boats in the harbour, the people and the smiles are real. There are no forced smiles pasted on for the tourists. All they ask is to be treated with respect and allowed to go about their regular business in peace. An island friend confessed that she had once impatiently duped one insensitive visitor, although she was a bit ashamed of herself later. "I was dulsing out at Dark Harbour and I saw one coming," she said. "He had that stupid hat with all the pins on it and a great big camera round his neck. He saw I was busy, and I was tired and fed up with all the questions and just wanted him to go away." When he asked her "Say, where do they do that dulsing anyway?" she said she just couldn't help herself. She pointed to the top of the cliff. "Up there," she said. "Up there!" the tourist exclaimed. "Then why do they need boats?" "Oh, they throw the dulse down to the bottom and the boats collect it down below," she invented cheerfully and walked away leaving him scanning the high cliff for impossible seaweed activity. At least the naturalists would have known better than to look any further than the intertidal zone.

As before, our group spread out around the various holiday accommodations and inevitably we passed on gossip and information that we gleaned from other tourists as we went along. It seemed that there were snob values depending on location. Everyone loved Maude and Gerald Hunter's 'Cliff by the Sea' cottages beyond Seal Cove, and the coterie of faithful who went there year after year became a special clan who clung to their lovely site as their special Paradise on Earth. Linda L'Aventure and Cecilia Bowden's 'Compass Rose' was mentioned as special in all *The Places to Stay in Canada* booklets, but Kathryn Buckley's 'Inn at Whale Cove' on the Whistle Road had even greater panache. That establishment, and the from-away summer community that had built up around it, had the class distinction of the elite, enhanced by its fame as the summer refuge of American author Willa Cather.

My little Wilson cabins, modest in location and on any scale of elegance, could never compete with such splendour, yet I loved them and my hosts dearly. This time I stayed alone in the shore cabin, and from then on, every time I came, I asked to stay there. Jennie gave me such a warm welcome on arrival, and Eldred, who was always tinkering and modernizing the cabins, kindly said he would never alter a stick of my shore-side cabin as long as I loved it the way it was. I wonder how he reconciled his beliefs with my terrible habit of drinking wine and putting a candle in a green bottle beside my jar of wildflowers to sit by the gentle glow and watch the lights over the harbour at night, Eldred who was a staunch Baptist and member of the Gideon Society that puts Bibles in every tourist room in North America, and who went with Preston Wilcox to Fredericton every year to make protestations to the provincial government against the sale of wicked liquor on the island of Grand Manan.

The shore cabin was so small that I felt I could stretch out my arms and lean in any direction and touch a wall in each of the two tiny rooms. There was a small table with two chairs under the harbour-facing window and I would sit there and look out at the changing tides. From full sea to dark steaming mudflats, there always seemed to be something new and interesting to see. Although I don't remember ever going down on it, I had a miniature beach at my front door called 'Sisters'. There was a deck that went round on two sides of the cabin and I was tempted to sit out on the harbour side in a bathing suit and enjoy the morning sun until I realized the proximity of the guys working not far off at Grand Manan Boats. I might be a Stranger From Away, none stranger, but I owed it to my kind hosts to behave myself while I stayed on Grand Manan. In fact, I brought that swimsuit down every time I came, intending that 'this time' I would go swimming in the cold Atlantic water, but each time it went back home dry and unused.

My friend Ralph Hoskins stayed at Grand Harbour Inn, where Liz Jennaway was only too happy to spoil him, and together we explored the island, photographing wildflowers as we often did back at home, and trying not to get cross with our other naturalist friends, Muriel and Fraser Cliff, whenever we met up with them somewhere along the way. It seemed that no matter what wondrous thing we had found that we wanted to report, they had always seen something better, and it began to grate on our nerves. They had one announcement that gave us a shout of laughter, however. "Have you seen the notice on the way to Dark Harbour?" they asked eagerly. "The Dark Harbour Cliff and Country Club?" Indeed we had, and been told that it was an in-joke thing for some pretty active drinking parties at the top of that so-called dulse cliff. "Well," said Muriel from her innocent Christian church background, "we stopped and told them our name was Cliff and asked if we could join!"

1980 was a wonderful year to get to know and really love Grand Manan. It was a time when islanders were happy with the way things were and the way they were going. We 'from-aways' who were wandering around in a Shangri-la of our own invention, admiring the place and people from our romantic emotional distance, might smile superiorly and say, "Of course Grand Manan is thirty years behind the rest of the world," before hastening to add that we liked it that way, but Grand Mananers knew that they were doing well and making progress built on what seemed then like a pretty solid foundation because the fishing had never been better. The new boats, the new gadgets, were all helping to bring in more and more fish, lobster and scallops, and prosperity smiled on every hand.

That was the era when the fishermen went up the Fundy on a Sunday afternoon to start a week of scalloping. I was on the wharf at North Head when I saw them all walk by with their stylish Adidas bags to take with them. A good-looking young couple walked past me, he with his bag and she in a red sleeveless dress that made me shiver because I was bundled up against the cold and she looked so unbelievably exposed.

They were having a hard time saying good-bye and took so long that eventually one of his mates yelled out to him. I loved his suitably nautical shout. "Come on then," he cried in exasperation, "she'll not rust in a week!"

When the scallopers came back, the catch was 'shocked' (i.e. shucked) in the harbours and the 'shockers' were paid good money to remove the edible muscle that was so prized in gourmet cooking. Eventually, the shells would be dumped on Castalia beach or at the Thoroughfare, or used to make firm beds for roads that would stink to high heaven until the remaining rotting animal parts would finally make peace with their burial grounds. This inshore shucking practice would shortly be banned when it was decided that it was necessary to protect the small scallops in the beds below the fishing areas, and from then on the work had to be done on board the boats up the Bay.

After our group went back to Montreal on that second visit, I came back on my own to stay. At that time, my husband was often travelling abroad, my older son had left home, and my younger son was frequently not at home, either. On my own, suddenly I would have the feeling that I simply had to get back to the sea, and I would jump in the car and head eastwards, through the lovely Eastern Townships to Cookshire and then along a strange hilly road that ran parallel above the northern border of New Hampshire, a road so straight that one could imagine the original surveyors standing on hilltop after hilltop marking their immaculate lines, until at Notre Dame de Woburn I turned southwards, down the mountainous Maine trail that once had formed the trek of ~~Matthew~~ Benedict Arnold's ragged army heading north to conquer Quebec City. Impossible to drive that road without imagining those tired men struggling to move heavy canons and equipment over that difficult terrain, farm boys who had been conscripted out of nowhere, dressed so inadequately that some of them arrived in a Quebec winter without shoes. From ski country to farm country I went southwards, until at Skowhegan I turned east for Bangor and the skyline drive to Calais, and finally across the border into Canada where suddenly I was an hour behind New Brunswick time. Sometimes in St. Andrews I visited Randi Olsen or Mike and Noreen Butler, whom we had met through our weeks at the Huntsman, sometimes I just raced for the ferry or stayed at the Whites' B&B in Blacks Harbour. However I did it, I can't remember how many times I came in the next year or so, either alone or with one or two friends, and at the Wilsons' assortment of housing I think I must have stayed in every one.

Dorie McNiven and I shared the log cabin on one occasion. While I pottered around vaguely, Dorie went about purposefully collecting fruit for her home-made jellies and organizing Grand Mananers to collect for her in future. I first met this amazing woman when Elizabeth Parnis and I were giving non-credit evening classes in 'Edible Wild Plants' at Macdonald College and Dorie was one of our students. We learned then that she was a descendant of Peter Redpath, the sugar robber-baron as she called him, and had inherited a huge property in the Laurentian Mountains north of Montreal and needed money to pay the taxes so she could save it for her children. Dorie learned everything we taught her about the edible wild fruits of Eastern Canada, and was soon off and running, building up her 'Wild Thyme' cottage industry and selling her jams and jellies at every country fair she could reach in the country. It was not very long before her jars were being sold at the counter of the Toyers' Ferry Wharf Inn.

On one never-to-be-forgotten Thanksgiving weekend, I came to the island with Keith and Shirley Rourke. We drove all night through Maine, admiring the beauty of the fall leaves highlighted by Keith's bright new headlights, and on the ferry over we were rewarded by the extraordinary sight of a large whale swimming very close alongside, so close that everyone inside watched it with amazement, as it seemed to be watching us. I knew so little about whales at the time that I can't remember giving it a name but I think it must have been a humpback. All I remember is a large eye in that huge body and what looked like a smile on its face. At the Wilsons, I think we stayed in the cabin by the driveway, an upside down sort of place with living area upstairs and bedrooms down below, and Jenny took us over to the Grand Harbour Baptist Church on the corner to show us the nautical Thanksgiving decorations, a wonderful, colourful harvest of the sea, with lobsters, sardines and dulse, and figures in hip boots and sou'westers plying their oars near the altar.

With Isabelle Lafrenière, we stayed in the trailer. Isabelle, a delightful French-Canadian real estate broker from Westmount, was a keen member of the Montreal Field Naturalists Club, as well as recently belonging to the Cat Nats. "Just think," she confided, with her wonderful throaty chuckle, "on my sixtieth birthday I am going canoeing! What my non-naturalist friends will think of that!" She was ecstatic about everything on island. She loved all the fresh seafood and finding someone who could give her real home-smoked haddock, and with her new-found birding zest she loved going out with Preston Wilcox to see the "pouFINS". She was so enthusiastic about the latter that for years afterwards Preston would ask after her, and when her daughter came to the island many years later and mentioned her mother to him, she got a special welcome in memory of that earlier happy trip to Machias Seal.

Even when not with Isabelle, every trip to the island always began with a drive down to Seal Cove to see Preston and book a trip out to visit the puffins. His wife Pearla would be sitting there knitting and I bought my good thick hiking socks from her while Preston let me know when next he could take me out. One day she looked up from her knitting and regarded me with something uncomfortably close to scorn. "I wouldn't pay good money to go out to see them birds," she said severely. "Not me!" It was an interesting opinion in view of her husband's occupation, but Preston and I just looked at each other and grinned.

It was because of Pearla that I had my first adventure with gulls eggs. When I arrived at the house in Seal Cove that day, Preston had just brought her back from collecting some on Wood Island and she kindly gave me one to try. "Cook it longer than you would a hen's egg," she advised. "You'll find the yolk is very orange and the white is kinda grey but they're some good." I felt quite privileged to be given this chance to do as the islanders do, remembering wildlife official Robie Tufts' story of accosting two Grand Mananers who had been doing it illegally, and when he slapped one man's side in a purposefully friendly way, the pockets ran orange with broken yolks.

I took the large speckled egg back to the cabin and put it in the fridge. The next morning I took it out and looked at it. "I'll have it for lunch," I decided, putting it back. At lunch

I decided to have it for dinner. At dinner it seemed a good idea to leave it for breakfast tomorrow.

These continued acts of cowardice went on until the day arrived when I knew I had to see Pearla again. I took out the egg at breakfast time and put it in water to boil. I cooked it for twenty minutes. "Maybe I'll give it another twenty minutes," I decided. After forty minutes, it didn't seem a bad idea to make it sixty. There was no way this egg was going to be under-done! Meanwhile, I poured out some orange juice and set the table as prettily as possible to maintain the façade of normacy. When the hour was up, I scooped the egg into an egg-cup, set it on the table and sat down. None too bravely, I raised the spoon and cracked the shell open. There was a sort of empty sound to the cracking, because it seems that Pearla had gathered the egg just too late in the season. Inside was a very well cooked, very dead, baby gull. "You know," someone in Montreal told me later, "they would consider that a delicacy in the Philippines." I did not. It took me several years later, when Bernard Lorimer brought me some fresh ones, for me to try gulls eggs again, and I found that Pearla was right. It took a bit of getting used to the orange yolk and grey 'white', and this time I did not cook them so long, but to me they tasted exactly like hen's eggs, which I've always considered 'some good'.

All of this did not change the fact that going out to Machias Seal with Preston was always the highlight of my many first visits. His boat carried eighteen passengers, and we would all line up at Seal Cove fishing wharf as he brought the pristine white-painted *Senorita,* cleaned up from its non-puffin occupation of fishing for lobster, to a small floating dock below. The height of the tide made a big difference as to how far down we had to go to reach the boat, but it was always an exciting moment as we clambered on board to sit on the back-to-back bench in the middle and move away out of the shelter of the harbour. I loved the sound of the engine as it went out through Seal Cove Sound and along the southern shore. There were no salmon cages then, nothing but a few isolated herring weirs and the sea enclosed by Inner and Outer Wood Islands, sea stretching out to Gannet Rock Light and the line of treacherous off-shore shoals that were only visible at low tide, and sea ahead to another rock that was Machias Seal way out there in the middle of nowhere. Gulls flew from island to island, guillemots dived and swam to avoid the boat, a salty spray splashed up to wet our faces. We were glad of warm outer covering and I of Pearla's socks when the air rose up from the cold ocean waves.

We could always warm up in the cuddy, although Preston, as always, spoke little as he stood at the wheel looking straight ahead. When we reached Machias Seal, going close to the shore past even smaller Gull Rock where we sometimes saw seals, he stopped the engine and we found ourselves looking at a flat islet with little else but a lighthouse, a cluster of working sheds, and three small houses, two of them red-roofed newer bungalows and one the black-roofed keeper's house of previous decades. There was no real landing place, merely a gully running between a rusting metal slipway and seaweed covered rocks, so in order to get ashore Preston pulled up the dory that he had dragged behind us in the wake and proceeded to lower his passengers inside, a few at a time, taking several trips to row us all ashore.

We were helped up onto the runway by the lighthouse keepers and Canadian Wildlife summer students who were there to tell us all about the puffins. Hundreds of terns screamed overhead, staccato screams that tore holes in the sky and were known to do the same to unprotected human heads, for these birds meant business as they dived in protection of their young. "Most of them are Arctic Terns," we were told, "the longest migratory flyers in the world." Thanks to the oceanic influence of the cold Labrador current, Machias Seal was about their most southerly nesting area. The majority of them nested in the Arctic but they all flew south in winter to the Antarctic bottom of the world.

The terns laid their eggs in loosely-constructed hints of nests on the open surface of the land, one or two at a time, but the puffins tucked their solitary eggs down in a crevice or burrow on the rocky western side. Razor-billed Auks shared this area with the puffins, standing erect like dignified head-waiters while their funny cousins played comedian to their straight-man routines. We were not allowed to visit the north end of the island where there were a few musty-smelling underground nests of Leach's Petrels, but we could go out to the puffin blinds a few people at a time, taking care not to tread on a tern nest or chick along the way. Inside the blind, we peeked out eagerly at curious puffins who looked back at us, heads on one side, observing us as strange creatures, too, and there was always a moment of excitement when a new puffin arrived, flapping its ridiculously small wings furiously and landing with an awkward plop, all the time with a row of fish hanging neatly out of its mouth. The puffins sometimes landed on the roof of the blind, and there was something quite delightful about the role reversal of being underneath as they shuffled noisily around above us as if we were in a burrow and they were on land overhead.

On my many trips out to see the puffins, I befriended the wife of one of the keepers. Preston was responsible for taking all the supplies out to Machias Seal at that time, and on one of my trips he brought Maggie back with her young children to visit her family. She was a nice girl and we stayed in touch by letter afterwards. Because of this friendship, on another of my Grand Manan visits when Preston had to go out on an errand but the weather was too foggy for his regular tourists, he said he would take me out alone to see her. He will never know how thrilled I was to be given this honour, though perhaps if he had looked back at my joyful face as I leaned over the rail exulting in the salt spray he would have guessed and given his reserved smile of approval.

His errand was to pick up some men from the Canadian Wildlife Service who were conducting the annual marine bird survey. I had only a little time with Maggie before having to jump back on board. Preston was taking them to Kent Island so we took a more southerly course across a sea that was as flat as a pane of glass. Shrouded in fog, there was nothing to see, so I sat and talked to a pleasant man who seemed to be the leader of the group. "Do you come out often to do this?" I asked him. "Er – no," he said. Seconds later, he bolted for the side of the boat and violently vomited the entire contents of his morning stomach. I had the feeling that this was going to be his first and very last marine bird survey at Machias Seal.

White Head, Whales and Geese

There was only one time when I came to the island on holiday that I did not stay at the Wilsons'. This time, there was no room in any of the cabins, so I moved up the road to Grand Harbour Inn. I knew Liz Jennaway from Macdonald College, where she spent the winter months teaching. She was a whiz with fabrics and the art of dyeing and I was always too intimidated by the chemistry to take her courses, but by then I was also working at the college, teaching Botany labs and helping out in the Herbarium as well as continuing to teach non-credit evening courses in 'Edible Wild Plants', helped by Helga Seifert when Elizabeth Parnis left us for Toronto. I was working, too, on a new course that was to be called 'Medicinal Plants', picking my way sceptically through a rocky path of herbal claims, trying to decide which cures were suspicious and which could be believable.

On this trip, I was collecting and pressing plants for the herbarium, so when Liz gave me a room at the top of the house, I set about finding a way to dry them in the damp island air. I took the screen out of the window and propped it up on pieces of furniture to sit above a lighted lamp that I put down on the floor. Over it, making sure the screen was strong enough to hold them, I stacked the presses with the drying material. It worked very well and I was delighted with the results, but amused to learn that my hostess and her staff found this so extraordinary that they were leading guided tours upstairs to have a look when I wasn't around.

It was around this time that I began to come at different times of the year because I was also collecting plants near

St. Andrews. Dr. Carl Medcof, whom we had met and very much enjoyed during our club field trips at the Huntsman, had heard that I was connected to the McGill Herbarium and asked if I would consider looking at the flora of nearby Sam Orr's Pond. This was not one pond but several, ranging from freshwater to increasing saltwater depending on distance from or proximity to the tidal shore. The local marine biologists often used the ponds for comparing the sticklebacks that were affected by the changes in water salinity, and Mike Butler, who had been our excellent and delightful leader for our Huntsman stays, took me out to have another look at them. From then on, for several trips east, the pattern of my time was to visit Mike and Noreen Butler and family in St. Andrews, spend a few hours at Sam Orr's, and then head off for the ferry to Grand Manan. I kept this up for many months, over a year or even two, I think, until the last time I went to the site. To my horror, when I got there, I found that a holiday house had been built at the end and the shore-side pond was filled with floating toys and rubbish. I never went back, but I am delighted to hear that it has been acquired by the Canadian Conservation Council and restored to its original purity.

During the period of going to Sam Orr's Pond, two more Cat Nat members, Alan and Tineke Hipkins, came with me for early spring collecting and afterwards we left for the island as usual. On one of our days together on Grand Manan, when the sun was shining and the wind was calm, we decided to go to adjacent White Head Island, reached by a twenty-minute ferry ride off the southeast corner of the main island. "If Grand Manan is the end of the world," a White Header once told me, "then White Head is falling right off the end of the world." The *Lady Whitehead* ferry was away to be serviced so we went out from Ingalls Head on Lester Carroll's boat. A pretty young teacher in a flowered summer dress went over with us, on her way to the elementary school there, and when we docked, intending to just walk around, Lester forever endeared himself to the Hipkins by offering us his car to drive around the island for the day. What is it about White Head, apart from the nice inhabitants, that is so special? There is, of course, the striking feature of the Head itself, gleaming white in the sun as Samuel de Champlain found and named it. Bigger than Machias Seal, it is about the size of Anchorage Park, and the one main road can be travelled east to where it meets the Bay of Fundy at Gull Cove, or west to where it divides, north to the Head or south to where it looks out to the Atlantic Ocean from a beach of fossil tree-stumps, carrying on out to the lighthouse and a sandy beach where practically no one ever goes, out to where the everlasting fog rolls in that can envelop the island for days and weeks at a time. The island's main claim to international fame comes from a celebrated visitor, John James Audubon, who stayed with pioneer William Frankland in 1833 and is reputed to have worked on his Elephant Portfolio portrait of the Herring Gull that then nested most unusually in White Head Island trees.

The next time that I went to White Head was with Jane Smith, also a Cat Nat and colleague at the college. We went to see Linwood Carroll, Lester's father, whom the Hipkins and I had met when we returned the car. Dear Linwood, then the oldest inhabitant of the island, was completely bewitched by Jane. He couldn't get over this competent, confident Englishwoman who knew all about gardens, could cook and sew and paint and repair houses, and had even once run a garage and knew all about how to fix cars. He dressed himself up smartly for us and allowed us to take him for a picnic at Gull Cove, and forever afterwards corresponded with us happily in letters covered with religious stickers proclaiming his faithful love of God.

On the beach that day, Jane searched for pebbles that resembled 'something', unlike me who always just loved them for their feel or varied colouration, and she found one that looked to her like a seal. That Christmas, she gave me a strange little parcel that was marked "It's not a seal, it's a puffin." By then I had forgotten all about her rock but when I opened it up there it was, the bottom of the original seal turned around and now it was the head of a splendid new species with a brightly-painted big orange bill.

It was at the Wilson's cabins that I first met another White Header, albeit one who had been living away for many years. I was staying in the little shore cabin when a small toddler headed determinedly past me, looking if he was about to fall headlong over the rocks onto Sisters' Beach. I persuaded little Ryan to take my hand and go back to his grandfather, which was how I met Tim Cossaboom and we became summer friends. If our paths crossed on future visits, he would invite me in for tea and I would enjoy learning more about his childhood on White Head. Often these visits would be interrupted by a phone call or another visitor and I would wave good-bye and go back to my own domain.

As time went on, I learned that Tim had a divorced wife and adult children living on and off Grand Manan, and a second wife and small daughter living in Bad Salzuflen, Germany, and he was trying to divide his time between the two abodes. He had bought an old house on the Thoroughfare Road for his Grand Manan family, but they had moved out and he was now very anxious to sell it. One day he took me to see it. The old wooden house, built in 1902, stood foursquare to the winds at the head of the harbour. On the west side, the land bordered a tidal brook, overhung by a large willow tree. A wide verandah circled the house on the brook and harbour sides. Everything looked neglected but beautiful. There was a lot of dark wood inside but the rooms, surprisingly small but with high ceilings, were airy and bright. Most of the windows were tall although two of them were smaller and were inset with coloured glass panels that had obviously been chosen with care. "You have a lovely house, Tim," I told him. "Would you like to buy it?" he asked with a wry grin, and I laughed because we both knew it was impossible.

When we talked, I did not tell Tim much about my life in Montreal because, although he had travelled considerably, I knew he would not understand. It was so far out of his experience of living, this White Header who had finished his schooling at the one-room school where he had been in a class of four, who had grown up with boats and fishing and dulsing with his father and grandfather who had both died when he was young, who had all these present family complications and now seemed to live in a Neverland of not quite belonging in two places at once, but none of this background belonged in the world of Field Naturalists and Plant Science and the friends and city people I knew. So I just talked about his world and we left it at that, comfortably, until I came back to the island to say "hi" if he was there and we could just pick up where we had left off over a cup of tea.

Back in Montreal, between my holiday escapes, I would catch up with the friends who had been with me on the various trips east and resume a busy life where there was never a shortage of things to do. Not only was I active at the college, but I was putting in a week a month working as editor of the Catherine Traill Naturalists Club newsletter. With a constantly travelling husband, the club was a very important part of my life. I enjoyed the people and interesting evening lectures and most especially the field trips close to home as well as afar. Every month we went out with an expert to look at the world around us, at forest, bog and meadow life, learning as we went, and it was all incredibly exciting for someone who until then had only known the joys of city living.

We were reaching out to other clubs in the area, too, so I found myself botanizing *en francais* with the delightful members of SAJIB, the amateur botany club at the Montreal Botanical Gardens. Among the trips I took with them was one with Isabelle Lafrenière and other members to a lichen and seaweed course on the north shore of the St. Lawrence just west of Tadoussac. All the others were doing the lichen study, which meant that they kept regular hours and mealtimes, but of course my trips to Grand Manan had made me interested in seaweeds and in my course we had to go with the tides. What fun we had along the shore, doing transepts to collect the marine algae from lowest to highest heights of tideline, seaweeds that we brought back to a lab and pressed. Since the entire course was in French, I usually fell on Isabelle's shoulders and babbled in English whenever I saw her, but we both had a wonderful time.

Some of us Cat Nats went to Tadoussac on a whale-watching trip with the Montreal Field Naturalists Club. Dorie McNiven drove us along the south shore of the St. Lawrence to Rimouski where we were to go out on an old tugboat, the S.S. *Metridia,* docked in the harbour some ten to fifteen feet below us when we arrived. To get down, we had to climb up onto a concrete parapet and go straight down a perpendicular gangplank. It was not a regular gangplank with steps. It had only narrow slats for a footing and a wonky rope to cling to on one side. The others went down easily, but I have always had trouble with heights and I stood at the top and panicked. "I can't do it!" I cried. Two crew members tried in vain to persuade me to let them help me but no matter how hard they tried I couldn't face that step out into uneasy space. "Look, let me wait until the tide comes in and it won't be so far down," I said miserably, and when that didn't work I just sat in the car and cried that I was going to take the bus home. Eventually, the crewmen came back. Very gently, they walked me round the harbour to a small boat moored by the ramp. Over the harbour we went to climb up over another boat moored beside our tug, and from there I jumped on board into the arms of dear Bill Reynolds, the longtime Chairman of the Field Nats club, who somehow managed to make me feel welcome instead of the world's silliest fool.

The boat beside us left early the next morning but soon returned to port. It was a wild and windy day and we were to hear later that it was on that same day that a boatload of young people drowned going out to Ile Bonaventure from Gaspé not far along the coast. Our captain decided to run straight to the other side of the St. Lawrence where he could hug the northern shore going west towards Tadoussac. Although I have crossed the Atlantic several times, I have never been on such a rolling boat. Into the water the *Metridia* rolled to one side, coming up splashing, only to roll over to the other side without pause. Wave after nasty wave crossed our bow, where of course I was standing getting seawater in my camera bag, looking out over a heaving, foaming, grey sea where it was totally impossible to even think of seeing whales, but it was my turn to be the one who was enjoying it. Bill very soon turned green and all around me people were being sick but as long as I turned my head away and stayed outside I was fine. It was a very relieved group of people who scrambled happily off the boat at Tadoussac. "Aren't you coming, Wendy?" they asked. "Er-in a minute," I said. When they had all gone, I practised going up and down that gangplank until I knew every inch of the boarded slats and every wobble of the flimsy rope rail. Only then did I climb ashore, knowing that I would be able to get back aboard without repeating my earlier disgrace. The next day was calm and clear and we went up the Saguenay to see belugas, and out in the St. Lawrence we saw minke and sei and three blue whales and it was heaven. Now when I returned to Grand Manan, I would be anxious to go out looking for Atlantic right whales, when I knew there would be no treacherous gangplank to deal with on the island!

A Field Nats trip with leader Ben Lapin was to Cap Tourmente, about thirty miles east of Quebec City along the north shore, to see the migrating Greater Snow Geese. The world authority on waterfowl, Peter Scott, called this annual event "the greatest goose spectacle in the world" and it certainly lived up to his recommendation. The time to go was the third weekend in October, a time of the greatest concentration of birds and also a time when the hunters were not allowed inside the reserve. I went with Elizabeth Parnis and Keith and Shirley Rourke and we left Ben's group to walk along the railway track and go down to the shore where we sat in awe, watching hundreds of thousands of these large white birds feeding close at hand, necks yellowed with mud from their search for the roots of American bulrush, *Scirpus americanus*, that sedge that marks the place where the sea and river water runs brackish instead of becoming salt. When a small plane flew over, the entire flock rose in the air, and it was as if all the Greater Snow Geese in the world had disappeared forever, until slowly they came back, skein after wonderful skein, in lines and V's and straggles, to land again on the beach beside and beyond us, their brilliant white plumage gleaming against the dark sky and water, backed by the glowing colours of late fall. After that, although it was not nearly so impressive, the Rourkes and I went to see the Snow Geese on the other side of the river in spring, travelling from Montmagny to St. Jean Port Joli to find small groups of geese against the grey of piled-up winter ice-floes, and if I use the Canadian route to or from Grand Manan in the early time of year I still always look for fields of white near Montmagny before 'les oies blanches' head north for the summer.

Closer to home one summer, some of us joined a birding trip with the PQSPB, Montreal's excellent birding society, and were led by Judge Montgomery southeast of Montreal to the Sorel Isles in the St. Lawrence River. We went out in a small open boat, landed and hiked across the flat meadowland in search of birds. Well, most of us were looking for birds, but I had been taking a fascinating course at the college in grasses, sedges and rushes with Marcia Waterway, and here on this tiny islet we were surrounded by everything I had been studying. It is never a good idea to look at anything else when you are with people who are birding, but I'm afraid it was irresistible even if the judge never spoke to me again. By the time I reached the shore where everyone else was standing, I found two people trying to decide about the strange-looking tree I had become, with my brown jacket and pants topped by a green backpack out of which waved a canopy of collected green plants.

The day turned violent on that shore. We were looking out towards the skyscrapers of downtown Montreal as a thunderstorm blew in and the whole shore became a drama of wild skies and peculiar colours, whipping wind and water, and then the thunder and lightning and onset of a downpour of rain. As we walked back across the meadow in the drenching shower, I was behind Ralph Hoskins. "I hope you realize," he said solemnly, as Ralph so often did, "that we are walking across here with metal tripod conductors and I am the tallest person here." "That's why I'm walking behind you, Ralph," I told him. "I reckon the lightning will get you first!"

That was the summer that I went back on my own to the little shore cabin on Grand Manan in August. I collected sedges and rushes on the island, too, only I wasn't as successful with drying them and they were all mouldy when I got back home. Tim had visitors from Germany and I went with them on the Southern Head trail. We did not get very far however. A little past the pond they panicked, because the trails were not the wide gentle walking paths they were used to in Europe. "The trees, they are so close, the path it is not so good, we could be lost, we must turn back," they said, and so we did. I think Tim hoped that they would buy the Thoroughfare house but it was not long before they were gone.

That was the visit when Tim's older son, Brian, and his wife, Sue, kindly took me up to the top of Beech Hill to see the view over Long Island Bay, a lovely view of little companion islands stringing southwards from Long Island to the three

Ducks. These were the Grand Manan archipelago islets east of Nantucket and then northeast of Ross and Cheney and White Head Islands, joining with the main island to make an incomplete triangle in the sea.

Just before I left the island to go home, Tim's younger son, Liege, and a friend showed up at the door of the shore cabin. "We've brought you lobsters to take back to Montreal," they said. They refused to take any payment, and maybe Tim had already paid them without telling me, but I thought it was a wonderful gift from these two nice teenagers. I was expecting Colin to be home from his business activities overseas or elsewhere in Canada and at least this was something he would appreciate from the island to which I could never persuade him to come. It was high summer as I drove home in the heat and although the lobsters were sitting in a bed of seaweed I kept stopping to buy ice to keep them cool. By the time I reached home I would have given anything to find a nearby ocean in which to put them, but by then, of course, it was much too late.

It can only have been a couple of weeks later that I received a phone call from Tim. He had had bad news from Germany and he was going back to Bad Salzuflen in a hurry. His lovely wife, Crystal, had been diagnosed with cancer and he wanted to get home before they operated on her. Even more terrible news followed almost immediately afterwards. Tim had his ticket ready to leave when his beautiful son, Liege, the one who had been so kind to me with the lobsters, was killed while working under his car. He had taken off the wheels but neglected to use blocks to hold up the vehicle, relying on a jack that had failed. Fortunately, he had died instantly, but I looked out my window at the driveway where my sons had so often worked on their old jalopies and I wanted to sit down and cry forever.

Tim was staying on the island for the funeral, he told me, and then he was leaving at once to go home to whatever faced him there. His news over that winter became more and more grim as time went on. He wrote of Crystal's operation for cancer and the difficult conclusion of the doctor that there was no hope to save her as it had progressed too far. She grew increasingly weaker until she died in January, when there was a big funeral because she had been a much loved pharmacist in the town.

As if all this sorrow had not been enough, a short time later he wrote with the additional bad news that his daughter Andrea had been found to have a severe curvature of the spine, so severe that the German specialists wanted to put a steel rod down it and have her lying on her back for a year. I wrote back begging him to get a second opinion, and he contacted the Children's Hospital in Toronto where he found a doctor who was working on a new and better treatment that would involve putting in two smaller rods and she would be able to walk around almost immediately. When they came over for her operation later that year, I was able to get up to Toronto and meet Andrea for the first time. She was a lovely girl, very gentle and loving with a confident mind of her own. She was already able to get around a little and in no time at all she was up and away, for she was used to being active and independent. The only thing she was forbidden to do was to jump on a trampoline, Tim said happily, so news from Bad Salzuflen was more cheerful from then on.

Audubon and Alligators

Back in Montreal, when I was not answering the siren call of Swallowtail to come back and smell the sea on Grand Manan, I continued to enjoy my life in my pleasant West Island suburb with friendly neighbours, and I loved driving west to Ste. Anne de Bellevue to participate with enthusiasm at the meetings or field trips with the Catherine Traill Naturalists Club, or to work in that corner of Macdonald College that was given over to wonderful sheets of dried plants arranged in unnatural poses that were somehow reminiscent of Audubon's artistically arranged dead birds. I felt like I belonged very happily in this world, and I remember telling one of my lab students that I'd probably still be there when her children came to take their degrees at the college. But time has a habit of bringing changes, especially unexpected life-style changes for which we are never really prepared.

Both of our sons were married within a year of each other. Older son, Tony, was first, bringing home a girl he had met in Edmonton, and I was thrilled when Jeannine wanted to adapt my wedding dress for her bridal gown. I had had it made in London, England, when I lived there, with a jacket with long Juliet sleeves to be worn over a strapless gown with a circle skirt with yards and yards of ivory brocade from Oxford Street. When Colin and I were married in a little Air Force church in Scotland, the dress and I walked down a piece of the blue carpet that had been laid at Westminster Abbey for the Queen's coronation. I wore the same dress, sans jacket but with a long blue-green satin stole, to a dance in Aberdeen after our wedding, dancing all night with dashing men in kilts who plied Colin with chasers of whiskey until he could hardly stand up, and it was worn again by a sophisticated friend in Montreal who added elegant elbow-length gloves to go to a ball for Princess Margaret. Jeannine cut the wide skirt down to a straight one and added a sleeveless summery top and she looked absolutely beautiful.

Before the wedding, younger son John persuaded us that we should have a flute solo played during the service by his new girlfriend, Kim. A year later, he and Kim were married in a lovely ceremony in Lachine, and it was while they were still on their honeymoon that my husband and I decided to end our own marriage of twenty-five years, a decision that was difficult and painful at the time but really proved to be the best thing for both of us in the long run. Colin took an apartment downtown and I stayed on in the house.

I did not go down to Grand Manan that summer, but headed east all the same. I went with Isabelle Lafrenière to what was billed as 'Audubon's Labrador', a section of the north shore of the lower St. Lawrence River that the famous naturalist/artist had explored in 1833 after he stopped to look at the tree-nesting gulls on White Head Island. Isabelle and I drove to Sept Iles to meet the trip organizers, Kathy Blanchard of the Atlantic Center for the Environment, a charming redhead who was passionately devoted to her work in the lower St. Lawrence and Newfoundland, and Nathalie Zinger, a delightful graduate of Macdonald College who was now working for the Quebec Labrador Foundation. In the hotel and airport we met the rest of the group. We all fit comfortably into one van, and from there we drove to Havre St. Pierre where the road ended at that time. On the way, they told us they had something special to show us and we stopped to look at the huge carcass of a beached blue whale, reeking horribly.

Marg Elliot and I shared a motel room that first night, and it was one of the most uncomfortable nights of my life. The window screen was obviously not doing its job and the room was thick with mosquitoes. We tried everything to get rid of them, using pillows to hit the walls as we did not want to disturb our neighbours, but still they buzzed around us. We laughed a great deal at all our antics but by 4 a.m. we still had not been able to sleep. I sat up in bed reading trip literature with the bedding covering everything but my face while Marg decided that since she was going to be bitten anyway she might as well go out and look at birds.

From Havre St. Pierre we went out to the Mingan Islands, recently turned into a provincial reserve park, and here we began to see the influence of the cold estuarine waters. The islands were small and very similar to Machias Seal, except that they were mostly rocky and the vegetation was low-grown or absent so it was easy to see the tern nests everywhere. It could be only a short visit as we had further to go that day, flying in two little planes to go east, and then picking up a fishing boat to take us to the Ste. Marie Islands near Harrington Harbour. These were the islands that were well known to Allan Moses, Grand Manan's famous birdman, when he worked as warden for the Labrador Patrol in the summer of 1923. They were beautiful, unspoiled, green and hilly gems of islands, and with the strong sub-Arctic element of the cold surrounding waters I was soon seeing many of the plants I had last seen in the cemetery at Frobisher Bay. It was also a haven for northern marine birds, and we visited the nesting areas of terns and guillemots and puffins while we wandered over the same kind of heavenly tundra terrain we had walked on so long ago on Baffin Island. I never wanted to leave again.

There was something familiar about the lighthouse keeper's house and sheds, with the standard red roofs of the Canadian Coast Guard structures. It had been arranged that we would spend the night in the empty house of the keeper, using our sleeping bags on the upstairs floors, men in one room and women in the other, but Isabelle and I and one other person opted to do things differently. People who snore do not like to be billeted in dormitories! It is so embarrassing to disturb other people who are trying to sleep. Snoring jokes aside, it is so difficult to offend people you would not offend if you were awake. Producer/director/poet/writer Pierre Perrault opted to sleep under the dining room table, Isabelle chose the kitchen floor, and I, who had spent the day collecting wonderful sub-Arctic plants for the Herbarium, chose to keep working in the pantry where I could keep a light on until I was too tired to continue. Eventually, I turned out the light and opened the door, and I too settled down to sleep and snore happily, with my head in the pantry and my legs stretched out in the kitchen.

On the noisy fishing boat en route to Harrington Harbour the next morning, I stood next to Pierre Perrault. He was a very imposing man and an ardent separatist who believed passionately in the protectionism and pride of his people. It was a time in Quebec when we were all taking sides on this issue, and those of us who were English but loved Quebec and the Quebecois people were always in a particularly difficult position. We did not often have a chance to talk directly to a French-speaking separatist, so I struggled to tell him, in his beautiful language that I could only massacre, how I understood his deep feelings of nationalism but worried that separatism would isolate his people, cut them off and not give them a chance to grow, and I feared for them because I loved them, too. At the end of a rather emotional exchange, Pierre suddenly smiled. "We will give you a passport to our new country, Wendy," he said graciously, and with that the discussion was over.

Harrington Harbour was a wonderful island place with no real roads, only wooden walkways between the houses, wide enough to pull a cart, and a church that was sometimes Anglican, sometimes something else, depending on what kind of minister arrived there. "It's all the same God," our hostess told Marg and me in the house where we were billeted, which was refreshingly different to hear. I loved seeing the little Arctic flora on the island but I didn't collect plants because I knew Dr. Swales had been here once and collected extensively. She had come in a little two-seater plane from Sept Iles, and laughed when she remembered that when they got up in the air the pilot had said thoughtfully, "I wonder how you fly this thing?" "I'm sure I don't know," said Dr. Swales primly, "but I hope you find out soon."

It was four o'clock in the morning two nights later when 'The Boat' that ferried everyone and everything along the endless north shore arrived at Harrington Harbour and it was time for us all to go on board. We noticed that despite this bleak middle-of-the-night hour, the islanders were waiting to do their banking business at a window with a grill inside the boat. Our group chose to take over an isolated upper cabin on the top deck and made ourselves comfortable there for the entire trip, except that at each port along the way, while passengers and freight were loaded and off-loaded along with truckloads of commercial white bread, I would run ashore and see if there were any plants worth collecting before the warning whistle blew to announce the boat's departure.

The sun came out as we went along and Pierre Perrault came and sat beside me on the outer deck and told me something of the history of the places we were passing, places with wonderful names like Tête-a-la-Baleine, Baie-des-Ha-Ha, and Bonne Espérance, and said that when Jacques Cartier came along this shore he was not the first because he asked directions of fishermen who were already there from the other side of the Atlantic. He gave me a copy of his beautiful book, *Toutes Isles,* which I read as I sat there in the sun. As we neared the outermost northern section of the Gulf of St. Lawrence, the sun began to set on the horizon, and we went down for supper. We noticed that the steward was wetting the tablecloths, a sure sign of rough water to come. Pierre Morency, our other well-known Quebec poet/writer travel companion, had been sick on every conveyance to date, so we called out to him "Pierre, it's St. Jean Baptiste Day, how about a song?" From then until we landed in Blanc Sablon, all the Quebecois members of our group sang French songs in the upper cabin, Pierre with his beautiful voice never seeming to notice how rough it became.

In the hotel in Blanc Sablon when we finally arrived after midnight, Marg and I seemed destined to have another disturbed night when I heard a faint giggle and turned to find her lying with head down and feet in the air in a bed that had quietly collapsed at the top. It was 1 a.m before we had fixed it and could try to get some sleep. We went out the next morning to Ile aux Perroquets,. another small puffin island just out in the harbour, where the puffins nested in burrows that looked very different from Machias Seal because of the cover of grass. The naturalist who accompanied us took one out of its burrow for us to examine close-up details of its face and bill. It was not a very happy puffin as it lay on its back in an ignominious position, and it made a growling sound like a cross little dog before it was put back safely below.

At L'Anse-au-Loup at the end of the Labrador road, we had one glimpse of an iceberg in the Strait of Belle Isle before we flew back westwards to the point where we could pick up the road again in Chevery. We spent our last night in the airport motel. I could not sleep, so I rose early and spread all my plant collection sheets on the reception floor to dry. Unfortunately, I had forgotten about the possibility of arriving planes. When one arrived, I hastily gathered up my specimens, but the passengers were interested, and before long we were all sitting on the floor looking at my little flowers. I was hearing a lot of "*C'est cute ça!*" when one man stood up to leave. As he passed, he patted me on the head, and I thought, oh, dear, people only do that to children or village idiots and I have a vague idea which one he thinks I am.

Just before our group parted for the last time in Sept Iles, we passed a cottongrass bog. White fluffs of this wonderful sedge waved and wafted in the wind as far as the eye could see. Several people jumped out of our vehicle and collected armfuls to take home, but what I treasure most is the solitary one brought back to me by Pierre Perrault. I have it still, pressed in the book that he gave me, before we said goodbye.

That winter I was working full-time in the Herbarium as Assistant Curator for Marcia Waterway who was still at the college but working on her PhD at Cornell University. Dr. Swales was also coming in every day and working over a viewing microscope, although it is hard to imagine how she saw anything of the minute plant details as she was already developing eye cataracts. She was great fun to work with, always cheerful and interested, full of encouragement and funny stories. One of them I remember was about a colleague who was notorious for being forgetful. He had come in to the Herbarium to tell her he was going down to McGill for something and she asked him if he would pick up some aquatic plants for her for a lab the next day. He said he would put a knot in his handkerchief to remind him, but when he pulled it out there was one already there. "I wonder what that's for?" he puzzled, so she didn't have much faith that he would do as he promised.

In the Herbarium and at home, Dr. Swales was much in demand for identification of Arctic plants. Unfortunately, when it came time for her to have the cataract operation it was not entirely satisfactory and she was never able to do fine work with the microscope again. It was very sad because it had been her life's work and she dearly loved it. She told me once that she kept having a recurring dream in which there was a patch of wildflowers in the distance but she could never get out to see them close at hand. I felt very bereft without her wise advice and happy company at the college, although I went to see her often at home and sometimes we went for drives to her favourite places on Ile Perrot or up in the Laurentian Mountains near Lachute.

When Christmas came that year, I was very busy correcting plant collections for the students in my lab and it sort of crept up on me. John and Kim came to stay with me after taking me to several of their friends' Christmas Eve parties. When we arrived home in the wee hours, they said, "Let's open our presents now!" I had not had time to wrap their presents so I didn't think this was a good idea at all but when they insisted, I went downstairs to get their loot and quickly grabbed something else. We proceeded to exchange gifts solemnly, they by handing out a beautifully wrapped package to each other or to me, and me by handing them in turn a paper bag. John has never let me forget the Christmas when I wasn't ready.

Because I was on my own that Christmas, I had already let myself in for an adventure with the Wildlife Resources Department. The students came to me early in December and asked if I would like to go with them to canoe with alligators in Okefenoke Swamp. Me? Canoe with alligators? Certainly not! "Oh, please," they begged, "we have to have two staff members or we can't go and no one wants to go because of Christmas." So of course in the end I relented, once again wondering what on earth I was doing when I knew full well that for one reluctant and unqualified adventurer it would be an uncomfortable and probably terrifying excursion.

We left on Boxing Day in one van and one station wagon and did not stop until we reached the park headquarters in Georgia. While the others went inside, I walked down to a pond with one of the students and we stood and looked at a huge alligator lying there with its eyes closed. "What would you do," I asked the boy, "if that thing opened its eyes and went for us?" Ask a silly question. "Lady," he said, "I don't know about you, but if that thing moves the first thing I'm going to do is shit in my pants and the next is to get the hell out of here as fast as I can go!" We were still contemplating this monster thoughtfully when the others came out with long faces. “We can’t go canoeing in Okefenoke,” they cried. “It’s been so cold that the frost has heaved up all the trails.” I tried very hard to look as disappointed as they did, but the leader caught my eye and grinned.

It was decided that we would head down to Florida “where it would be warmer” and we would have another chance. “Where it would be warmer” became our talisman of hope as we travelled southwards, always to where it was never quite warm enough. We went out from somewhere on the Gulf of Mexico to look for manatees, and camped at a survival-type campsite further south where some of the students were chased by feral pigs. We had a thunderstorm overnight in that strange forested place. There is something utterly terrifying about being in a tiny tent, in the middle of nowhere, with thunder and lightning on the outside of something as fragile as a nylon shell.

Most of us had canned salmon sandwiches for lunch the next day, while a smaller group had tuna because they arrived late. On the way south to Ding Darling park, someone cried “Stop the van!” and he raced outside and was sick. It was not long before someone else did the same thing. By the time we had set up our tents in various parts of the campground and sat around a welcoming fire, our numbers were considerably reduced. It was New Year’s Eve and we were supposed to be celebrating, but I remember that by eleven o’clock I was sitting in the women’s washroom with one of the girls and we were both as grey as the concrete walls. At midnight, the tuna crowd were the only ones left, and they went around being disgustingly cheerful wishing all the world a great new year. When they reached my tent, I could not even whisper, and I heard someone say "Why are we saying Happy New Year to an empty tent?" before they moved away. By morning, most of the ones who had been sick earlier were well enough to go to Sanibel Island to look for birds and shells while the 'sickies' stayed behind to recover. When we went over later in the station wagon, all I remember of Sanibel is a white fog, and when we got back, one of my lab students put her hands on either side of my head and gently laid me down on the seat to sleep. When I woke up, I was fine again and so were we all. As we continued down the road to the Everglades, we heard that the seafood company in question was recalling all its canned salmon because of the danger of salmonella poisoning.

At the camping area in the Everglades, the danger of canoeing with alligators reared its ugly head again. Half the group were going to look for hawks with the other staff member and the other half wanted me to go with them in the canoes. "You don't want me, I snore," I told them dismissively, but they said if I snored they would kick my head in and I was going with them. So I went.

We left early, and as the sun rose we were rewarded by the sight of a cougar crossing the road in front of us, moving slowly and deliberately until it blended silently into the woods on the other side as if it had never existed. When we reached the area to pick up our canoes, there were nine of us to be installed, three to each craft, and I was one of the ones to sit in the middle and be paddled along in luxury through the narrow water channels between the encroaching mangrove roots. It was rather disappointing to see no signs of life, until we found one small alligator sunning itself on a bank about a foot above our canoes. The student in the bow of our canoe wanted to get close to photograph it. I remember his saying to the boy behind me, who was still paddling, while he got his camera ready, "Closer. Closer. Closer... Too close, back off!" but I don't remember that the alligator did much more than move position and then settle back to sleep again. We never saw another one.

Our destination for that night was a 'chickee', an island platform in the middle of the Everglades lake, built by the park in imitation of the Seminole Indians who had created this form of living away from the mosquitoes near the shore. There were actually two covered platforms in this place, joined by a v-shaped runway that held a Johnny-on-the-spot toilet in the centre. The other platform was already occupied, or I might have gone over to snore alone away from everybody, but we all settled down on the same one for the night, the students in a puppy-huddle near the railing at one end and I as far away as I could get, near the picnic table and the runway to the toilet.

It was cold in the night and I kept snuggling down and down into my sleeping bag. At some point in doing this, I opened my eyes. Where was I? Why was there no roof overhead? Cautiously, I took my hand out of the sleeping bag and felt one side of the narrow runway and then the other one. There was no railing and the water was about four feet down. In my wriggling, I had managed to get quite a way down without falling off the side. Wide awake and somewhat panicky now, I wriggled back to the safety of the platform and clung to the leg of the picnic table before I sat up and looked around. Behind me were all those lovely kids, soundly sleeping, with no idea how lovely they were, and ahead of me was the lake and the low vegetation on the shore, while Venus shone as brightly as the moon, casting her light in a line across the water. I remember feeling incredibly lucky, to begin my fiftieth year to heaven in such a wonderful place.

When I got back from the Florida trip, I found another student waiting for me at home. I had decided to advertise at the college for a boarder to help out with house expenses. The first answer came from a delightful girl whom I would have loved to have had but fortunately for her and unfortunately for me she found accommodation closer to school. Another girl applied, a cold and difficult one whom I was very happy not to have, and then a tall, slightly older but still young Agriculture student named Jean Lepage showed up before Christmas. He told me he came from a big family on a farm near Rimouski, Quebec, one of twelve children who had all been named as if they were twins, so Jean was followed by Jeannette and so on as each boy and girl arrived in turn. It was agreed that we would share the house for meals and some mutual social activities, but we would keep our lives separate in personal ways. I was not to enter his room in the basement, nor to ask questions if he brought his girlfriend back with him from time to time. He did not smoke pot or drink heavily and he needed quiet in order to study.

Since he seemed like a nice person and I was going to be away during the holidays when he wanted to move in, it was logical to give him a key to the house, but after he had gone I suddenly panicked. I had given the key to my house to a perfect stranger! What did I really know about this seemingly innocent young man? I rushed to see the college registrar who laughed at me. "He's a very nice guy," she said. "He comes in here often when we have to straighten out his forms."

He turned out to be a very good and very proper boarder and I enjoyed having him to stay, but having had grown sons and their many friends around, I was quite unprepared for the disapproval that letting Jean live in the house would bring me. A few of the neighbours raised eyebrows until they got to know him, my mother was shocked until she got used to the idea, and it was obvious from the stiff tone in Tim's letters from Germany that he did not think my student arrangement was quite respectable.

My English mother-in-law was scandalized. "I would NEVER allow a MAN to live in my house," she wrote witheringly, "and a FRENCHMAN to boot!" I read her letter aloud to Jean in the kitchen while he strutted around trying unsuccessfully to look seductive in Maurice Chevalier style until we collapsed with laughter at the whole improbable scenario.

A Quiet Vacation?

It would seem from all my naturalist travels to faraway places that I had completely forgotten about Grand Manan, but I thought about it often and wondered when I would have a chance to get back. Tim was still in Germany and I heard from him quite frequently, but they were not letters with news, they were lecture letters, giving me no picture of his life in Bad Salzuflen, no word of how Andrea was getting on or what was happening with his family on the island. They were mostly disapproving comments about my life in Montreal or on my travels, taken from what he misunderstood from my descriptions. I began to feel rather like a Hagar cartoon I had once seen where the couple were depicted as walking down a road with the wife commenting on how beautiful everything looked while he glanced back over his shoulder and saw the whole world as crooked.

So it came as rather a surprise to get a phone call from Tim from Machias Seal Island that summer. He was visiting his son, Brian, who had taken the job of head lighthouse keeper, assisted by his wife, Sue. The second keeper's house was empty and only nominally furnished but it was usable. Would I like to come and stay there for a quiet holiday away from my busy life in Montreal?

A week with friends on a puffin island! What naturalist could resist such a temptation? Of course I immediately said yes. There would not be time to get to Grand Manan and go out with Preston so it was arranged that I would go out with a fisherman from Bucks Harbor in Maine. I would drive to Ken's house, spend the night there, and go out with him early the next morning. And by the way, would I bring food, as Brian was always hungry? Every phone call before I left reminded me to bring more groceries, but since he did not tell me what to buy I ended up bringing a ton of stuff that turned out to be quite unsuitable, except possibly cigarettes for Tim.

It was foggy when I got down to the coast at the end of a long day's drive. Darkness added to the confusion, and in Bucks Harbor I simply could not find the fisherman's house. There was only one house with a light on anywhere in the whole place, so in desperation I knocked on the door at midnight. The man inside was kind enough to get in his car and take me to my destination. Not many hours later, long before dawn, Ken put all my bags of groceries into his truck, shocked at how much I was taking, and drove me down to the dock. Climbing gingerly aboard, I tried not to notice that this was the dirtiest boat I had ever seen. We set off eastwards, not talking much over the roar of the engine, until the noise stopped and we were there.

Machias Seal! I could hardly believe how lucky I was to be going to stay there! What amounted to a small crowd by normal standards was waiting at the landing area. I had expected to see Tim, and Brian and Sue, and two Canadian Wildlife officials, but what were two RCMP officers also doing there? Tim would explain to me later but first, everything was handed ashore, everyone waved as Ken departed, then all the bags were carried up either to my house or the other one, depending on contents. We never saw Ken again. As the week went on and he didn't appear to tend to his traps as usual, Tim and Brian began to get worried about him. Eventually, the news got back to us that his engine had caught on fire on his way home, and he was only saved by other fishermen in the area who put out the fire and towed his boat back to the dock, lending credence to the old belief that it was unlucky to have a woman on board a working boat.

Tim had furnished the empty house of the second keeper with the bare essentials – a metal bed in one bedroom, an old couch, deck chair, table and chairs and lobster crate in the living room, perfect in its simplicity. I set out my camera, field glasses, plant press, and books, and began to make myself at home, imagining all the time I would have to read and dream quietly here, and how I could look at the flora and birds at my leisure.

When Tim popped over for a visit, there was much to be explained about what was happening on Machias Seal Island. This was July 1984, and the Canadian Wildlife Service had been monitoring the arrival of tourists from Grand Manan and Maine, noting the effect on the tern population. In their wisdom, they had decided that the number of tourists should be cut down. Preston, who brought eighteen passengers, must now bring only fifteen, and Barna Norton, who came out from Jonesport or Cutler, should reduce his passengers from fifteen to twelve. "That's crazy!" I exclaimed. "That's their livelihood. That's the capacity of their boats. And if you keep people together when they land, what difference does three more people make? It makes the same disturbance to the terns if one person walks down to see to the generator as twenty people walking together!"

Barna Norton, it appeared, certainly thought it was crazy. Moreover, he was an American citizen, he had been coming out to Machias Seal all his life without interference, AND he could prove that the island wasn't Canadian at all because it had once belonged to one of his ancestors. There was no way that he would agree to these stupid new regulations. When he arrived later that day with his usual number of tourists, he came with Tim to my house for a visit. The RCMP officers, who were on the island to explain the new rule and order Barna to comply, were staying at the other house and sent word that they wanted him to go up and talk to them. Barna exploded. "If they want to talk to me they can come here," he said. "I'm not a Canadian citizen. I'm not going to bow down to anyone in a red coat!"

He went back to Maine in high dudgeon after the RCMP left by helicopter, unfortunately killing a tern that had nested too close to the landing pad. Barna immediately phoned the reporters to tell them of the injustices he was suffering on what he felt was U.S. territory. He told them that Canadian helicopters "routinely killed hundreds of terns" when they landed on the island. He took up the matter of island ownership with his Senator, and he and his son John began to cook up a scheme to challenge this act of perceived Canadian oppression.

Until his next visit, life settled down to a usual routine on the island. Preston came once with his smaller number of visitors and was surprised to see me there, but I had only a chance to wave a hello to him as he ferried them over in his dory and returned to the *Senorita* without coming ashore. Brian and Sue went about their keeper business, although there really was very little for them to do beyond tending to the generator and keeping the grass mowed. Sue dulsed in the landing gully when the tide was low, spreading her seaweed out to dry on the concrete helicopter pad, and showed me how she made her wonderful bread, or we simply sat in the sun together while Brian and Tim played chess. The Wildlife students, Steve and Bruce, busied themselves monitoring tern nests and looking after a Leach's petrel that had hit the light at night and was now recovering quite happily in a sneaker beside their wood stove. While everyone else was otherwise occupied, I enjoyed going down to the puffin blind or looking at the limited island flora and collecting what I could, or sometimes, when I did not have visitors, just sitting and looking at the sea and sky. The sun rose in the morning over the western cliffs of Grand Manan and set in the evening over the eastern coast of Maine. Puffins sat on the roofs of the sheds both early in the morning and as the sun went down, looking like a long line-up of big-headed old men, wise in years of puffin-living. They were never there when darkness fell, after which there were only the flying ghosts of terns picked up when the light rotated in their direction.

What is it about small islands, especially lighthouse islands, that is so magical? Is it the reduction in numbers, or the variety of numbers, in a space that the mind can encompass, let alone just see it whole? Machias Seal was only one kilometre by half a kilometre at low tide. Apart from the birds, there was nothing exceptional about it, merely a slight rise, barely above water level, clothed in rocks and tall wildflowers and the man-made structures that were linked to each other by wooden walkways. And of course there was the lighthouse, standing proudly over everything, the light barely visible by day but coming into its own at night.

Tim took me inside the lighthouse a day or two after I arrived. There have been one or even more Canadian lighthouses on Machias Seal since the first was erected in 1832, which in Canadian eyes establishes the island's claim to belonging to New Brunswick and not Maine, although the international boundary line has never been clearly delineated. It might seem to be rather silly to be arguing over which country owns a dot of rock with a few puffins, but with offshore fishing rights and possible oil exploration, these little pieces of land can assume much greater proportions. I was visiting just around the time of the unhappy Falklands episode, with the television news full of the arrival there of a British warship, followed by images of dead British and Argentinian soldier boys lined up for burial side by side, so although I knew it was not at all probable, as I went inside the lighthouse that day it was not altogether surprising that I had a sudden shivery vision of Canadian and American warships towering over the little island of Machias Seal.

The ground floor at that time was empty, reminiscent of an earlier era when it had been a schoolhouse for as many as twelve children when a teacher came over in the summer months. We climbed up to a smaller landing and then to the light itself at the top level. Tim showed me how the light worked, with a beautifully calculated outer Fresnel lens, consisting of glass plates set at an angle, and a thousand watt bulb in the centre. Before I saw it, I had always imagined that lighthouse lights blinked, but now I saw that the light inside remained constant while the lens moved around it, arranging the times of the flash with the unique configuration of glass and metal.

Because I thought it would be romantic, I slept one night on the second floor of the lighthouse. Everyone thought I was crazy, which of course I was. Defiantly, I settled down with my sleeping bag, looking happily up at the marvellous light above, and thought this would be something to tell my grandchildren one day, but it was really rather cold and very uncomfortable on the cold hard surface and by 4 a.m. I got up stiffly and crept back to my bed in the house, sleeping until a very late breakfast, regardless of scorn of keeper and noise of tern.

When Tim had invited me for a quiet holiday on Machias Seal, he had neglected to tell me that the wheeling terns screamed incessantly day and night. When the fog rolled in, the foghorn joined the chorus, although I was lucky that it was still a time when it was located at the bottom end of the island and not like in later years when Chris Mills was there as keeper. In his book, *Vanishing Lights,* Chris described what it was like when the foghorn was re-located in the base of the lighthouse, a few feet from the bedroom I was sleeping in. He slept in a bedroom on the other side of the house, with a pillow over his head and earplugs in his ears because the noise was almost unbearable.

Tim had also not warned me that my door would open constantly with visitors. I could not explain that it was a lot quieter living in the city! Tim was there a lot of the time, or Brian would come down, also, from the other keeper house, or Steve or Bruce from Wildlife would arrive unannounced as they seemed to have a constant need to check frozen bird specimens or collect frozen food from the deep freeze in the basement. I never went down to the basement and now I wish I had because they said there was a water tank down there to collect runoff water from the roof, although Lawrence Benson has since told me that in his lighthouse days he used to have to clean off the roof for bird droppings and I would have been appalled at what I would have seen in the water down below. Our electricity for the houses and the lighthouse came from the generator situated in the large shed near the landing area, and it seemed that this was what needed the most attention from the keepers as they were always having to go down to check or fuel-feed it.

The day came when the second round of Barna's battle with Canada began. An Armada from Maine arrived in the form of John Norton in a fast boat containing a crew of TV reporters, so now I could add a film producer in my bathroom to my growing number of visitors. A small plane flew overhead, obligingly causing the entire population of terns to rise in the air for the cameras. Next, Preston arrived from Seal Cove with his mandatory fifteen passengers, whom Wildlife Official Steve Daniels greeted pleasantly as usual. Then Barna arrived in his regular passenger boat. As was usual between these two, Preston rowed over to help bring the other tourists ashore, but when he reached the landing area, Steve officiously did as he had been ordered. "I'm sorry, Captain Wilcox," he said, "but the captain of his own boat must bring his people ashore." Preston and I exchanged raised eyebrows as he took them back and returned to the *Senorita* without further comment.

John was allowed to go out and help his father. The full load of twelve passengers was duly landed under the watchful eyes of Steve and the television camera crew. Then came the triumphant denouement. Back went John for Barna and one extra passenger, a sober-looking lawyer from Maine. Barna sat at the back of the dory holding up an umbrella decorated with the Stars and Stripes. He was wearing an old hat that made him look like the reincarnation of President Harry Truman. When they reached shore, Steve stepped forward. "I'm sorry, Captain Norton," he said firmly, "but you have one too many passengers to land on Machias Seal Island."

Barna put down his national umbrella and stood up in the boat. He looked pleadingly at Steve, flung wide his arms with a fine sense of timing, and raised his voice as loud as he could. "Let my people land!" he cried passionately for the cameras. The cameras loved it.

When the television folks had gone home happy with their perfect story for the evening news, a triumphant Barna came in the house with us to wait for his legal passengers. Gleefully, he showed us the article about his earlier visit and the comment about the helicopter killing all the terns. There was no doubt about his sincere belief about island access and ownership, but we all knew that only one tern had been killed by the helicopter, one of a pair nesting right beside the helicopter pad. "That's a bit of an exaggeration isn't it, Barna?" I ventured cautiously. His eyes gleamed. "Well, maybe," he conceded, 'but you must admit, it's a million dollars worth of publicity!"

When all the players in the historic Maine invasion had gone home and life was peaceful once more, the Coast Guard helicopter arrived with new visitors, Tim's son-in-law from Halifax and daughter Andrea from Germany. Brian went out in the rowboat to get lobsters, and we had a wonderful meal of celebration. It was decided then that Tim and Andrea would come back with me to Maine when Barna came back. We would pick up my car in Bucks Harbour, and then we would all go up to Quebec City to see the Tall Ships before going on to Montreal, where I would put them on a bus for New York, from where they would fly to Germany.

When Barna arrived, it was not long before we were all on board for the return trip to Maine. However, instead of turning southwest as he normally did, he turned the wheel northwards, heading up to a tiny islet called North Rock that is nothing more than the rock for which it is named. Geologically, it is the third piece of the Machias Seal archipelago, which in turn is a smaller part of the Grand Manan archipelago. He stopped the engine and stood smartly by the rail for an official photograph to be taken. Now we could see the reason for the change in route. When Barna had left Machias Seal on his earlier visit with the lawyer, they had spray-painted North Rock with 'USA' in giant letters, and he wanted his photograph with it to be given to the reporters in Maine.

For the rest of his life, Barna returned to Machias Seal every fourth of July to re-plant the American flag on 'American' soil. He came as the self-styled President of Machias Seal Territory, with his son John, as Vice-President, and the lawyer as Treasurer, and together they held a solemn ceremony before departing cheerfully from their usurping Canadian friends. After Barna died, John scattered his ashes on the island, so that some part of this disputed territory always belongs to him. The episode left a legacy of indecision about the fate of the island, as well as the fishing rights around it in what is termed 'the grey zone', and prolonged perhaps forever the continued occupation by Canadian lighthouse keepers.

One always hopes for a solution, but in the meantime perhaps the last word should go back to an earlier international problem with a happy ending. When Jack Russell from Seal Cove was the keeper on Machias Seal Island many years earlier, he would hoist the American flag on the flagpole whenever he saw a tourist boat coming out from Maine. His superiors were horrified. "Jack, you can't do that!" they told him sternly. "This is a Canadian Coast Guard station, and the only flag that can fly on the flagpole is the Canadian flag!"

Jack did as he was told and the American flag never went on the flagpole again, but Jack was a Grand Mananer, and islanders are used to creative solutions, especially regarding government interference in their lives. When the next tourist boat came out from Maine, the flag with the Stars and Stripes was waving in the wind to greet them, but no one could argue with its placement, hung out as if to dry on his wife Rita's washing line!

In the Steps of Porsild

Another winter passed in the Herbarium in Ste. Anne de Bellevue. By now, I was working as Acting Curator while Marcia was away at Cornell University completing her PhD studies, and on my own after Dr. Swales had had her cataract operation. The time was coming, however, when my work there would have to come to an end. What was I going to do next? It seemed that in order to continue in any aspect of Botany or Natural Science, I would need a Master's degree.

John Bain, my Plant Science professor colleague, wanted me to do it in his field of Chemotaxonomy. "Nothing to it," he said. He would supervise me while I spent the summer collecting large and horrible thistles in the Georgian Bay area of Ontario. I would bring these back to a lab in the college and spend the winter hanging dripping pieces of paper on a clothesline in a dark room to analyze the chemical contents. I shook my head. "It's very kind of you to suggest it but I think I'm a little too old for that, John," I said sadly. Sadly because this would have kept me at the college that I loved, close to the Herbarium and the people that I loved.

Then an alternative came from the National Herbatium in Ottawa where I sometimes went on botanical errands. "You have an English and a Botany background," said Chief Botanist Ernie Brodo. "Why not do a biography of Erling Porsild? He was Chief Botanist here until 1967 and died in 1977 and no one has worked on him since." It seemed like an interesting project. At McGill, I approached the Geography Department and found warm encouragement from Professor Müller Wille, who had done his PhD on reindeer in Lapland and knew that

Porsild had been strongly associated with the Canadian Reindeer Project. By April, it was agreed that I would work on the first part of the biography, covering Erling Porsild's early reindeer years from 1926 to 1935.

Too late, Arch Jones from the Morgan Arboretum at Macdonald College passed me in the corridor and called me into his office. "How would you like to do your Master's on the Arboretum?" he asked. He pulled out a thick manuscript from his files and threw it at me. "Look, this is the work that Mayfield did in 1951. All you have to do is look at what we've done in the managed and unmanaged areas since then and compare the differences. There's your Master's!" It was terribly hard to just give the manuscript back to him and tell him I couldn't do it. If I hadn't already been committed elsewhere, I would have jumped at the opportunity to stay on at my beloved college and continue to work in the wonderful field of plant interpretation, 'botany from the skin out' as I liked to think of it. How many times in the challenging and sometimes difficult years that followed did I wish that I had simply backtracked and taken up Arch's offer!

Instead, it was good-bye to the college, good-bye to my dear Cat Nats, good-bye to my feet on safe ground and my head in a field that I knew and loved. It would even be good-bye to Grand Manan for a while because where I was going was not east but west and north to Yukon and Alaska and the Northwest Teritories, heading for reindeer country. However, I began my work almost immediately in Ottawa, going through the Porsild correspondence files in the National Herbarium. The staff were wonderfully helpful, giving me complete access with free xeroxing facilities. I worked happily away at sifting through familiar and unfamiliar information, grateful that most of the official letters had been written in the era of the typewriter and amazed at how quickly mail moved in those days. A few feet away from where I worked in the Herbarium basement, Fenja Brodo was doing what I called real scientific work in her corner. She was classifying craneflies, using specimens mounted with pins onto minute foam squares, and she spent hour after hour after hour patiently moving the mounts from one section of her space to another as she sorted them. Twenty-five years later she is still doing it, she tells me.

I kept trying to get a feel for the man I had never met. Dr. Swales knew him so I asked her what Porsild was like. "Oh, he was rather quiet and gruff and sometimes impatient," she said. "He smoked a pipe. He was primarily interested in the north, I think." She went on to tell me the story of going up to Ottawa to ask his help in identifying some of her more difficult Arctic species. He dismissed her curtly, saying he had no time, so she worked on them on her own until she reached one that she was completely unsure about. Not to be deterred from her quest, she went back to him. "I'm sorry to interrupt you when you're busy, Dr. Porsild," she said, "but could you tell me if this is _____?" and deliberately gave him a name she knew was wrong. "Of course not," Porsild snapped and gave her the right one. "Oh thank you, Dr. Porsild," she said sweetly. Mission accomplished. Dr. Swales was not born yesterday.

Ernie Brodo tells the story of seeing two people within the space of a fortnight who had each met Erling Porsild at a dinner party. The first person said, "I have just met the most disagreeable man. He sat next to me at a dinner party and he never said a word all night!" The second one said, "I have just met the most interesting man. He was so amusing and told such interesting stories about the North and he kept us in fits of laughter all evening." The secret undoubtedly lay in the conversation at the table and whether it was in Porsild's northern field of interest. His long-retired secretary talked of his wry sense of humour. She had told him once how she would love to go to Europe but was afraid of flying. He had taken out his pipe and smiled at her. "Well, Miss Harkness," he had replied, "you'll just have to find a plane that will take you there flying very l-o-w and s-l-o-w."

It was stories like this that filled in the research shadows for me, but the real feeling for background would come with my trip to the north. The arrangement with the Geography Department at McGill was that I would work alone on research in Ottawa, thanks to the financial assistance of an FCAR scholarship, and I would take some courses at the university in the fall and prepare an outline of my thesis for the next January. Meanwhile, I would also travel up to the north under a training grant from the Centre for Northern Studies at McGill in order to bring life to my archival studies.

I flew out to Edmonton to stay with Tony and Jeannine, and started my fieldwork by looking at material in the Edmonton University library. By now, I realized that the first part of Erling Porsild's biography, during the years of the reindeer investigation, would be closely tied in with his working partnership with his brother, Robert, or Bob as everyone called him. One of the librarians put me in contact with Bob's son, Axel, who kindly gave me an invaluable typewritten copy of his uncle's working journal from 1926 to 1928. From Edmonton, I went by bus to the start of the Alaska Highway where I met my good friend Erika Mothersill from Victoria and her cousin Marina Kratochwil from Vienna. This amazing road was still under construction in many places. We worried about damage to Erika's car, but the scenery was breathtaking. We stopped everywhere that had any connection with Porsild, making a stopover at Liard Hot Springs before entering the Yukon, and then spending a few days in Whitehorse. There was not much material in the Whitehorse library, but I had a delightful interview with Elly Porsild, Bob's widow, who by then was frail and elderly but still had her charming sense of humour.

From Whitehorse, we drove west through the magnificent mountainous region of Kluane, across the border into Alaska, and on to the end of the road at Fairbanks. Erika and Marina explored the town while I worked at the Elmer E. Rasmussen Library at the University of Alaska and had a wonderful day with Dr. Robert White, who kindly took me out to show me the difference between caribou and reindeer at their experimental farm, and to the deserted reindeer station at Cantwell where the Porsild brothers had begun their training in reindeer husbandry.

On our last day in Fairbanks, we three decided that we could not come all this way and not cross the Arctic Circle. Some time along the route north out of town, we realized that we needed to get gas and pulled into a small community that Marina described as "a one-horse town without the horse". The only man we saw there shook his head. "He's not here," he said of the garage man. "He's gone to Fairbanks to get gas." We could get gas some miles further north, he said, that place was always open. It was my turn to drive and it seemed as if we would never reach "that place that was always open", so it was a huge relief when we reached a busy gas and restaurant stop at last.

When we finally reached the Arctic Circle, there was nothing much to see except a huge sign where we could pose for the inevitable 'We were here' photograph. Beyond and around us, the wide and empty tundra stretched as far as we could see, pierced only by the north-south line of man-made road and oil pipe. It needed little imagination to think of it covered with migrating caribou as we remembered the concern everyone had had about the impediment to migration caused by the construction of that oil pipe, but there was nothing animal or even bird to be seen that day. On our way back, we were suddenly stopped by a barrier across the road in the middle of nowhere. We sat there puzzling until a small plane appeared and used the road as a landing strip; someone got out, a car came to collect him, the plane took off, the barrier went up, and the 'runway' became the main highway back to Fairbanks again.

From Fairbanks, we drove south to Anchorage via Denali Park where we slept in a tourist-adapted railway coach. It was in a tour bus at Denali Park that I saw my first grizzly bear in the wild. It was moving along slowly on the other side of a wide valley, the sun catching the ripples of its golden fur, and it was absolutely magnificent. The driver said we could not get out of the vehicle. "He would be here in seconds if he had a mind to," he told us. "You would not believe how fast he can move." They had had a few accidents lately so he was ordered to be cautious, but at the end of the road he let out two people who were going camping in the wild. With something like awe we watched them go, a young couple who looked smaller and smaller as they set off for the mountain in the distance with only a backpack and trust in their own safety.

Anchorage, with its colourful horticultural cabbages and a log cabin with a garden on its roof, was beautiful, as was the road going east past gleaming glaciers. We saw sled dogs being put through their paces at Tok, and everywhere on the road to the border we stopped at roadside diners where the food was ample and good. Our first destination once we re-crossed the Alaska/Yukon border was at Dawson, that run-down, gold-fevered town that still finds gold in incoming tourists and makes fun of itself as it relives the days of *White Fang* and 'The Cremation of Sam McGee'. The others had fun being tourists but I was glad when we left to head eastward to the start of the new Dawson Highway, where I tried every trucker in hopes of a lift north to Inuvik. Alas, it was not possible, so I had to go back to Whitehorse with Erika and Marina who left me there while they travelled on south to pick up the boat at Skagway for the coastal return home.

The stopover in Whitehorse was productive, however, as I found a nice girl from the McGill Geography Department living nearby who kindly drove me up the Canol Road where the Porsild brothers had botanized and worked as it was being built by US Army Engineers during World War II. From Whitehorse, I flew to Inuvik in a little plane that looked down on the tailings of gold diggings, like giant earthworms below, down into Old Crow where the nurse beside me got out to be met by what looked like the entire population, over the Mackenzie Mountains marked by the wandering tracks left by hundreds of migrating caribou, over the amazing Mackenzie River Delta gleaming in the sun, and down to land at Inuvik Airport where I was bitterly disappointed to find trees. Miserable trees, scrabbling for life on the edge of the tree line, when

I had hoped to be far enough north to stand on the open treeless tundra that I had so loved on Baffin Island.

Inuvik had not existed in the Porsilds' time, having been built when it was decided that Aklavik was no longer suitable. I wished there was a way to get to Aklavik where the brothers had actually lived, but could not find anyone to take me. Travelling anywhere in the North is not easy – it often depends on who and what you know and a sort of instant decision involving being ready and lucky to go where you want to go. And then you might end up going somewhere else. At least there was a chance that I would get to Reindeer Station, the place that the Porsilds had built and then waited and waited for the arrival of the three and a half thousand reindeer purchased for Canada in Alaska. The long delivery trek had taken five years to cross the Brooks Range, move along the north Alaskan coast to the Canadian border, and finally to the west and then the east side of the Mackenzie River delta. Bob and Elly Porsild left the station towards the end of the waiting period, but Erling Porsild had stayed on with mounting impatience until Canada's reindeer herd finally arrived in 1935. He has been quoted as saying that if they hadn't come when they did, someone would have taken him out of there in a box.

It had been arranged for me to stay at the Inuvik Scientific Resource Centre, where I was billeted with a group of archaeologists searching for evidence of long-ago human migration. They were an enthusiastic group that left early in the day to go out and look for bones and artifacts, which they brought back and cleaned at the station in the late afternoon and early evening sun. Meanwhile, I looked at what information I could find in the library and waited for transport down the delta. The Research Centre people had told me in a letter that if I wanted to go to Reindeer Station I should have a gun and license to shoot before I arrived, because "the bears were bad there this year," but this had not been possible. Now they wanted to send me there with the Fisheries people, who would leave me alone for a day and then come back for me. "Er – what about the bears?" I asked. Remembering the grizzly at Denali and knowing that the station was in ruins, there was no way I was going to be left out there alone. In the end, they sent me with their technician, who would take me out in the Research boat and stay with me for protection if needed.

We were no sooner out in the middle of the East Branch of the Mackenzie when Manny told me to take over steering, he wanted to drink his coffee. I was suspicious of this 'coffee' as I had a feeling it was heavily laced with alcohol. The feeling grew stronger when we got to Reindeer Station, and I went to take photographs and do the most nervous plant collecting in my life, while my erstwhile protector, a small slight man, put his puny gun down beside him and made himself comfortable on a collapsed building with his cigarettes, lunch and 'coffee', looking more and more relaxed as time went on.

Apart from feeling nervous about possible bears, it was very exciting to actually walk around the Reindeer Station that I had read so much about in my research. Each of the brothers, and the Norwegian reindeer herders and families, had had their own houses or cabins dotted around the hillside, and these were still more or less intact, although the doors and windows had gone. A larger building was the one that had collapsed. It was interesting to compare the different view of the delta from ground level after seeing it from the air. Little could be seen except the immediate enclosing foreground of river and banks of low trees, so there was no way that the Porsilds could have stood on a hillside and seen the huge herd approaching.

On our way back to town, Manny and I climbed a hillside to see if we could see more, but there was nothing to see but more of the same. It was interesting sitting there with him while he had a smoke, because his father had been a German submarine captain in the South Atlantic during World War II. So there we sat, looking down on the Mackenzie River, while my mind went back to his father's wartime when I lived on another river in Mackenzie, British Guiana, and everyone worried about those German U-boats sinking our Allied bauxite boats. Life is really circular, not linear, as we touch each other at different points, often quite unexpectedly.

I wanted very badly to see the present-day reindeer herd, which was no longer Government owned. The Nasogaluak brothers from Tuktoyaktuk and one other man now owned the herd, I was told, and it could be seen from the air. Manny offered to take me up in his small plane after work. Lulled by a false sense of security after having got through Reindeer Station safely, I agreed.

He picked me up in his truck one evening after supper and we drove to the town landing area and climbed inside his little two-seater. I should have known that flying with Manny would not be an everyday tame occasion. "Put your foot on the brake while I wind her up!" Manny yelled, heading for the propeller, and I did as I was told in terror that the thing might take off otherwise. "Oh darn," he said when we got in the air above the town, "we're out of gas."

We flew to the regular Inuvik airport so our craft could be re-fuelled, with Manny sitting on the top. With that hurdle over, we proceeded to fly north along the east side of the delta, heading for the Tuktoyaktuk peninsula, and now we could see what we had missed from travelling the East Branch at ground level. The delta was so beautiful from the air, giving me the sensation of flying over blue water lace-tatted with land into innumerable water-holes, with nesting swans in each small opening in the lace. "What's that building, Manny?" I was stupid enough to ask. "What?" he asked, tipping the plane over on its side so he could see what I was looking at. I did not ask again.

By the time we reached the coast, we had finally run out of trees. The wonderful moss and lichen tundra stretched out forever and I wanted so much to land and walk on it again. Manny turned eastward along the peninsula until we could see Atkinson Point below us. It had been a Hudson Bay post that the Porsild brothers had visited in their eastward exploration in 1927, and later one of the DEW Line radar stations that had been erected to give advance warning of aircraft or missile attack in the 1950s. Manny decided that he wanted to go down and have a look, so down we went to the level of the cottongrass, but everything was too overgrown for him to land so there would be no walking on that beautiful tundra.

East again we went, looking for reindeer, but we never found the herd, learning later that it had been moved far to the east of the peninsula at that time. We did find an offshoot herd, or so Manny said but it might have been caribou, and he took the plane down for me to photograph them. Down and round we went, down and round again and again, and all I have is a photograph of terrified animals racing across the tundra to get away from this terrible metal predator that was threatening them from the sky.

Resigned to disappointment, we turned back to Tuktoyaktuk and landed, for coffee and a potty stop, at the centre for northern oil exploration. It was close to midnight and the sun was hovering around the horizon, but before we went back to Inuvik, there was one more thing I wanted to see. I wanted to photograph Erling Porsild's 'pingo', the large ice-cored hill just to the west of the settlement that had recently been acquired as Canada's only Pingo National Park. Porsild had introduced this Greenland word into the literature when he wrote a scientific paper on these interesting geological formations.

Up we went again in the little plane, to fly towards the west before turning north to the coast where the pack-ice was coming in on the shore, around and back to turn inshore towards the pingo. Manny again went down almost to the level of the cottongrass and flew towards it while I took my picture, but he stayed there so long, heading straight for the hill, that I finally yelled "Manny, GO UP!" When we got up in the air, barely clearing the summit, I hit him. "You did that on purpose, just to scare me!" I scolded him. Manny grinned happily, his northern pilot reputation quite satisfied.

Back in Inuvik, I was ready to leave again, this time to fly south to Yellowknife and Winnipeg and home to Montreal. It had been interesting to see this other North and compare it with Baffin Island, but I had been very disappointed to spend the whole time in the 'Little Stick Country' below the tree-line instead of on the soft wide-open tundra that I had so loved on my trip to the north-east. Although I decided I liked Inuvik, with its sense of democratic independence that I had not found elsewhere, still I would carry home a sad image from the North everywhere of a symbolic little man weaving his way unsteadily to and from the local drinking establishment, of native teenagers on street corners with the same defiant look I had seen on the faces of English teenagers when there was no work for them, and of small strong women with round sad faces who were trying to hold their families together against sometimes hopeless odds.

The scenery was magnificent but it was man's country, I decided, and however hospitable and friendly it was in so many ways, I was tired of the roughness and danger of it all. What I found myself wanting all of a sudden was to go east again, east to the sea to where the land and the people were comfortable and familiar, east to snuggle down under a colourful hand-made quilt and be warm again, east to where I didn't have to think of bears when I went outside. It was time to go back to Grand Manan.

Return to Machias Seal

When I returned home from my Porsild summer, there were something like eleven letters waiting from Tim. His life in Germany had been very difficult for him ever since his wife died. He wanted to bring Andrea to live in Canada, but all her mother's relatives pleaded with him to let her finish school in Bad Salzuflen where they felt she belonged. Tim reluctantly agreed. They had been living in two floors of her grandmother's house, so it was decided that Andrea would move up to the top apartment while her aunt took over the middle flat, and Tim would leave her and come back alone. In Halifax, on his way to Grand Manan, he went into the Coast Guard office and asked if they could get him a ride to Machias Seal Island. They told him that Brian and Sue had left but would he be interested in the job of second keeper? He jumped at the offer. So he was there now and would I, could I, consider coming down to see him?

I almost didn't open Tim's letters because I was so cross with him for his written tirades about my presumed awful way of living, which included his silly suspicion that I was having an affair with my student boarder, but when I came to the ones that were postmarked from Maine I began to relent. I was tired after all my travels in the North, and yearned to get back to the sea. Perhaps if we met face to face, I could knock some sense into his fool head? It was already getting on for mid-August and it would not be long before I would have to start attending classes in the Geography Department at McGill, but perhaps there was just time for a quick trip east.

With his invitation, Tim had suggested that I contact Barna Norton before he made his last trip with his tourists. I called Barna in Jonesport and he said he would be happy to take me out if I came down at once. I could stay with them until he was ready to go. I had never met his wife, Beatrice, but when I arrived she could not have been kinder. She and her uncle took me with them to tend their family graves, I remember. I, whose family is scattered to the four winds, was fascinated as they weeded and talked as if this or that relative was still with them in a world that seemed to have stood still. I envied them their sense of rootedness, which was something that had also appealed to me about the people I had met on Grand Manan who knew exactly who they were and did not have far to go to see where they came from, unlike the ones I knew in the city whose family histories, like mine, were always from somewhere else.

Barna did not have much to say on the way out to Machias Seal. He seemed to be rather secretive about something and I wondered what he was up to this time, but it turned out that he and Tim had had many a heart-to-heart conversation during the summer and he had decided that my arrival would be a surprise. As we got close to the island, I could see that Tim and a new keeper were playing chess outside in the sunshine and they were so absorbed in the game that they had not noticed our approach. My little friend looked dreadful, desperately thin and old and sick as well as unshaven, but I have never forgotten the look on his face when he looked up and I saw the joy in his eyes. I think that was the moment when I knew I was committed to looking after this impossible man, and heaven only knew what that commitment would bring.

The new keeper was Wade Guptill, a bright and cheerful young man whose every second word began with 'f'. As one of the tourists said, "He sure calls it as he sees it, doesn't he!" Wade was fun. He called Tim 'Uncle Henry' and was obviously devoted to him. They played chess together for hours. One afternoon while I was there, they were hard at it when he looked up from the game and said, "That's strange, Uncle Henry. It's sunny. Why is the foghorn blowing?" "Er, that's not the foghorn, Wade," Tim said with some embarrassment. "That's Wendy, asleep down the corridor." We all have to be famous for something and fame of my snoring travels far.

One of the official activities of lighthouse keepers, I soon gathered, was to keep the station clean and painted. Wade and Tim painted every day it was fine. The earlier paint was never scraped off so the exterior was just given another layer, none too carefully over the lumps, coating them with shining white so that the whole resembled a winter ploughed field covered with snow. They painted everything, including themselves, until they came in covered in splatters in order to write in the official log that today they had done their duty. "Date _____, painted," was written in day after sunny day. It was once reckoned by someone that all the paint that was used in a year on Machias Seal would have been enough to paint the whole town of Saint John several times over but of course they reckoned without the many non-painting days when the island was obscured by wet fog.

Tim and Wade were both heavy smokers. Tim's favourite brand was Camels, because, he said, he had been lured by all the ads when he was growing up showing recommendations from doctors that this was the best cigarette to smoke. If they ran out before new supplies came in, there would be a desperate search for butt ends, tea leaves, anything they could possibly smoke, until their precious tobacco could be replaced.

Wade's idea of neatness did not exactly match that of his father, Sydney Guptill, who was a long-time keeper at Gannet Rock Lighthouse, southeast of Machias Seal, alternating monthly shifts with Don Denton. Those men were both neatniks. Every time there was a change, we would be sure to hear a call over the radio to someone on Grand Manan complaining about the mess the other had left behind, although in fact in either case it was always immaculate. One important aspect of the radio phone was the local weather conditions, and a report had to be given by the keepers each day. The weather news from Gannet was of particular value to the fishermen coming out of sheltered Seal Cove because things could change so much when they got out into the open waters. It was one of the reasons that everyone would later fight so hard to save Gannet Rock from being shut down, apart from the fact that it was the oldest lighthouse in the area, but the time would come when closure was inevitable for all our lighthouses except Machias Seal.

It was strange to be there without the Canadian Wildlife officers or all the tourists coming to see the puffins, but it was now late in the season. The birds usually arrive by the end of April and leave in mid-August. The adults go first, leaving their chicks in the burrows and waiting for them to come out overnight and join them in the water before they all go out to the open Atlantic. Before Barna returned on his very last trip to take me back, all the puffins seemed to have left, but there was one chick that had stayed behind. We found him wandering around on his own, looking confused. He was a funny little thing, still bright-eyed and curious but obviously very hungry. We tried him with canned sardines and he wolfed them down but we worried that we should have got him something fresh. The puzzle about why he was still there was partly solved when we put him in the bathtub and he sank like a stone. After he died, Wade and Tim sent his body for analysis and it was confirmed that his oil glands had not developed enough for him to survive in the ocean.

When Barna came back for me, Tim really wanted me to stay and it was hard to leave, but I knew I had to get back to the university. So back I went, leaving Machias Seal with difficulty, doing the long drive wearily back from the coast, moving from one world to another very different one, to start again at the place where I had taken my first degree.

It was an odd sensation to walk up the McGill campus that first September morning with the son of friends who had graduated with me thirty years earlier, while this young man whom I had known since he was a baby told me that he, too, was just starting a graduate programme. I was sixteen years old when I did that walk for the first time, fresh out of boarding school in England and as green as spring grass, but I had loved my years at McGill, loved everything about it, and I knew the old campus inch by inch – the curved gates on Sherbrooke Street where I had once been swept up unwillingly into a student protest riot and learned the terror and fascination of being carried away by mob rule, the road up from the gates where I had once stood with the entire university when Princess Elizabeth and Prince Philip had come to the college in 1951 and I had been only a few feet away from their open car, the statue of 'The Three Bares' as we called them when we sat on the grass beside them and had our lunch, the steps up to the Arts Building which was so often a meeting place beside the Grecian-styled columns, the old Redpath Library where we used to study in the high ceilinged great hall, the soccer field that used to become the site of the graduation ceremony in May. This was the same field where the graduates in my year were supposed to be when our time came around, except that it rained and the ceremony had to be held in the old Hockey Forum at Atwater, the Forum where the Rocket used to play, only it was just after the circus had been there and it still smelled of the elephants. So many memories, and all of them the kind that one wraps up in a quilted blanket and takes out now and then to cherish as part of what makes one richly alive.

So here I was all these years later, now I was an ancient fifty, and here I was starting again, looking at a campus with a lot more buildings, and all around me were the students younger than my sons. To say I was nervous was an understatement, but my professor, Ludger Müller Wille, who was younger than me, was extremely kind and understanding with his student who was so much older than the rest. I needed kindness because, unlike Macdonald College where everything had been horizontal and easy and friendly, everything at this new McGill was vertical and difficult and strange – steep hills that became icy and treacherous in winter, a tall, narrow Geography building where everything was up and down stairs or elevators, a cold place where everyone was a stranger and the work seemed to be hard to grasp. After the comfort of the college in Ste. Anne de Bellevue where people seemed to be talking a language I understood, I felt like a fish out of water with everyone using strange jargons and seeming to have such a different concept of the world that I thought I knew. How did Karl Marx get into Geography? It seemed that my old-fashioned thinking was linear and concrete while everyone else's was spatial and existentialist. How on earth was I going to fit in here?

We all find our own solutions to problems and mine was to just go with the flow until I could find my own niche. After all, I was no stranger to feeling different from everyone else after all the travels of my childhood, and slowly I began to feel that at least I could do what I came to do, which was to work on Erling Porsild. As background for his early life in Greenland and later in the reindeer years, Ludger had me reading literature about the North. I used to read in bed at night, all the stories of terrible circumstances of survival and non-survival written by and about grizzled men in parkas isolated in ice-bound ships, or wandering, starving, over the freezing tundra, until I complained that I was getting frostbite lying there under the covers. The seminars that I attended were all about aspects of the North. I soon found that as a group we were different from the other students in the department, who were working on maps or social problems or a host of other challenges that had somehow got linked together under the general heading of Geography, but I could be separated out even further into my lone field under the title of Historical Geography.

My work was now divided between going to the seminars at the university and driving up to Ottawa to work in the National Herbarium on the Porsild correspondence or the National Archives on the material for the Canadian Reindeer Project. When I worked at the Archives, I stayed at a B&B a few blocks away, and every morning I got up and had breakfast before walking over and falling into the Archives, and every night I left the Archives and walked back to fall into bed at the B&B. I was a bit nervous walking alone on the empty streets late at night and practised how I would act if someone followed me. "It doesn't matter what you do to me," I would say, with a sad and tragic air, "because I have AIDS." I wonder if anyone has ever used that truly terrible line? Because of my famous snoring, the owners kindly gave me a solitary room in the attic, and many mornings someone would come puffing up from the breakfast room in the basement with a message. "Wendy, your lighthouse is calling you!"

We had our first break at the university in October, and John and Kim and I decided that we would all go out to Machias Seal for Thanksgiving, taking the turkey and all the trimmings. We would go in two cars as they would have to get back to work. This time, we headed for Cutler, Maine, where a nice fisherman whose name I have forgotten had agreed to take us out. As we left the harbour early the next morning, the sun was shining and it was a beautiful sight looking back towards the land with two other fishing boats following on either side of our wake, but once we got out in the open sea it was rougher and rougher. The radio crackled with amused questions from the other fishermen. "How're your passengers holdin' up?" By then Kim was asleep standing up from all the anti-seasick pills she had taken and John was looking pretty green so I was glad for them when we turned back. They decided they had had enough and in any case were running out of time so they started on the trip home while I waited for the next chance to go out alone with our fisherman friend, hoping the uncooked turkey could stand the delay.

We left before dawn the next morning. Once outside the protection of the harbour we still rolled a little but not as much as on the previous day. As the light came up without the sun, my fisherman headed for his traps, and we searched for his white lobster buoys on a grey-white sea. To me, it was like searching for the proverbial needle in a haystack, because although I looked and looked I could never see them until we were right on top of them. Hauling the traps was cold, heavy work, and I decided there and then that whatever price we land-lubbers pay for lobster we should pay it and be grateful, because the fishermen who are out there in the cold and wind doing this hard work deserve all they can get and then some.

I also learned that one of my fondest illusions about their life at sea was completely erroneous. I had always imagined the fishermen all alone in the quiet of sea and sky, doing their job in silence and tranquility except for the sound of their engines, until they returned home to light and human noise ashore. I soon learned that my friend was anything but alone out there. During the whole trip out, until he had finished hauling his traps and dropped me off at Machias Seal, the radio crackled and shouted with gruff male chatter like a city taxi in rush hour.

Wade and Tim and I had a great Thanksgiving until the same fisherman came back to pick me up again, the only problem being that we had gone for a walk all around the outside of the island and I turned my ankle going over a puffin rock and sprained it painfully. Saying good-bye was not too hard because Tim had agreed to take time off and come up to Montreal in December. "See you at Christmas!" I called as I climbed into the dory with difficulty and waved as the fishing boat was pulling out from the shore.

He did come up to see me for Christmas but it was not exactly a roaring success. He had been very cold on the overnight train and had not slept a wink on the way up. He was not feeling very well. Always ignorant about such things, I was beginning to learn that Tim was a man with many medical problems, starting with neglected measles when he was young that had turned into rheumatoid arthritis and other complications. He had back problems and stomach problems and was often in pain so that it sometimes seemed a miracle that he was still alive. Always a heavy smoker, because he said it helped with the pain, he coughed and coughed, and he quickly went to bed instead of meeting the friends I had asked for dinner the first night. He pleaded sickness, but he really wasn't in the mood to meet strangers and he strongly disapproved of my serving wine at the table.

The question of alcohol became a subject for argument between us. I understood Tim's anti-drinking Baptist background, but he did not understand my feeling that it was all right if it was done properly. In vain did I try to explain that I believed it was perfectly all right to drink a glass of wine or beer with meals. "After all, Jesus drank wine when he broke bread with his disciples," I said, but Tim would never agree with me that moderation was the key. He had grown up believing that it was evil and sinful, he had seen too often the damage done to people's lives with drunkenness, and he worried about me because he was sure that even moderate drinking always led to abuse.

I think Tim did not know the meaning of moderation! Not in anything. He was an all-or-nothing man, impulsive to the nth degree, which made him both delightful and impossible to live with. As with so many problems between us, due to the way we had been brought up and our very different life experiences, Tim and I would never settle the large questions of who was right and who was wrong, so the best times were when they were never discussed.

He was not a great addition to Christmas celebrations on that visit either, because he did not believe in them. Generous to a fault at all other times of the year, he simply didn't believe in everyone going crazy at that one time of year when he felt it should be a quiet religious holiday. Much of his reservations went back to his problems of spending too much money on Christmas presents for his young family and going into debt because of it, so for him the whole feeling of the season was wrapped up in anger and guilt. I was so sorry that it was that way for him but there was no way that I could make it right. He did bring me a present, however, a watercolour that I loved, painted by a talented young Grand Manan teenager named Michael Field, showing a man in a dory laden with presents going out to a lighthouse island for Christmas.

After Tim left, I settled back to my Master's studies, but in March I packed up some of the Porsild papers, intending to do a lot of work while visiting Tim out on Machias Seal, and drove to Saint John where it had been arranged that I would go out in the Coast Guard helicopter. It was Jack Jardine who was my pilot flying out, pointing out a running moose in a clearing below and kindly refraining from playing his usual trick of frightening his passenger by pretending to have a heart attack in mid air, and I had my first sight of the little lighthouse island in winter. No birds, nothing but brown vegetation and buildings stark against a grey sea. Over to the east lay Grand Manan and the sun still rose over the cliffs but much further south than later in the year. It was wonderful.

Of course I didn't get much work done. It was much too hard to concentrate. Wade and Tim played a lot of chess and we all drank a lot of coffee and did a lot of talking about nothing in particular. "Weren't you lonely out there?" friends asked when I got back to Montreal. "Never," I told them, "I've been much lonelier in a crowded city than I ever felt on Machias Seal." I felt that I learned the lesson of the relativity of loneliness while being out on that lighthouse island. In the wide open space of sea and sky, it only needed one or two people to somehow fill it, people that one knew who were simply there, unlike the millions of unknown ghosts of busy cities who passed and scurried off to see someone closer somewhere else. Even being completely alone for a time was somehow less lonely, because in that space one could be self-contained.

When Tim's time as assistant keeper came to an end early in April, we piled all his belongings out on the grass. It looked a lot more sitting out there than it did inside, but it would be carried in a sling under the helicopter and delivered to Grand Manan that way. Not that it always arrived safely, judging by the story of Brian's pool table that was supposedly dropped somewhere on the back of the island where it must still lie in pieces! However, when Jack arrived, he yelled "No time for that! Weather's coming in and we have to get going!" Wade promised to bring in anything that would get ruined by the rain, so we just left it all where it stood, climbed aboard, and waved good-bye. Up, up and away we went, heading north up the Fundy, over North Rock and Campobello and Deer Island to Saint John, to pick up my car and head westward.

I would never see that little dot in the ocean looking the same way again. Soon after Tim and then Wade and Tim's replacement, Blake Morse, left, the Coast Guard became serious about what would happen on Machias Seal. No more families, no more haphazard running of the place. No more furniture strewn around on the grass for the helicopter to pick up or deliver. There would be two houses only, one for the Canadian Wildlife Service and one to be shared by two keepers, officially furnished for their use. The keepers would come for one month at a time, bringing their food supplies with them, and then be replaced by two more when the helicopter returned. They were less likely to be Grand Mananers and more likely to be men from Nova Scotia who had served long terms on lighthouses that were now closed. The big generator and the foghorn were moved to the ground floor of the lighthouse and the old keeper's house and all the sheds were burned down.

I have been out once to see the changes with Preston's son Peter, who took over the puffin trips to Machias Seal when his father retired. Without the old keeper house and the auxiliary buildings near the landing, the island looked smaller than ever. The puffins were there in the same numbers and so were the terns dive-bombing overhead, and the birds were just as magical as ever, but I wondered where the puffins sat at night now there were no more shed roofs for them to perch on. I was glad I had seen Machias Seal when I did.

Endings and Beginnings

When Tim came to live with me in Montreal, he kept asking about important papers he had sent to me a long time ago. "You never did what I asked you to do," he accused. "Tim, I don't know what you're talking about," I said. "I never received any papers, honestly. Are you sure you didn't send them to Andrea?" "I sent them to you," he said bitterly. "Can't trust you with anything."

Some time afterwards, a thick envelope fell through the mail slot in the front door. Tim picked it up. "What's this letter doing addressed to you in my handwriting?" he queried, as if I would know. When we opened it up, there was a note from the post office on Campobello Island explaining that the letter had been found in a bottle that had recently washed ashore. Then Tim remembered. Back on Machias Seal the previous fall, he had seen a Maine fisherman hauling traps close by and hastily put all his papers into an envelope addressed to me. He put this into an empty coffee jar, threw in some money to cover the postage and time involved, screwed the jar tight, then he went down to the shore and called to the fisherman before throwing the container out to him. He watched as it floated out in the direction of the boat. "I thought the man heard me," Tim now remembered, "but he suddenly gunned his engine and was gone, the blighter. Imagine that jar turning up on Campobello all these months later!"

Of course, he never said he was sorry for being so nasty to me about my supposed negligence, but I was starting to learn that this was what it was going to be like sharing a life with Tim. At least I was bigger than he was! This was the man

I had been describing to everyone as kind and gentle? Hah! This was the man who as a brash young fellow in Boston had gone into a full bar on St. Patrick's Day and called loudly "Why is an Irishman like a banana?" Green-beer filled glasses stopped in mid-air and the whole place stilled to listen. Tim completed the riddle triumphantly. "Born green, lives yellow, dies rotten!" he shouted. For a minute, the shock in the Irish-insulted silence was palpable, until the big bartender, a good friend of his who was standing behind the counter as shocked as everybody else, suddenly threw back his head and roared with laughter. The room broke up, everyone chugging and chuckling, but it was less at the offensive joke and more at the audacity of this cheeky youngster who looked so small and thin that a light breeze would blow him away. The bartender took Tim to one side afterwards and shook him roughly on the shoulder. "Don't you EVER do anything like that EVER again," he said. "You're damn lucky to be alive."

All that summer, Tim pottered around my Pointe Claire house 'fixing' things. This usually meant that I had to 'fix', too. The more difficult the job, the more impossible it seemed, the more he liked the challenge and the more uncomfortable positions I found myself in. "I can't stand up there, I'll get giddy!" I wailed. "Up you go," was the unsympathetic response. "Bring me a such and such," he would order later, and I began to learn the mysteries of screws and screwdrivers that seemed to have been invented by a gang of rival builders who made sure that every tool and part had a different name and shape and no one fitted another.

Everything with Tim was a new learning experience for me. We went to the open market to buy tomato plants for the garden. I was looking over the selection of flats for healthy plants about a foot high without paying attention to what Tim was doing. Suddenly I noticed four green trees walking in the direction of the car. "Good heavens, Tim," I said when I caught up with him and the girl from a nearby stall, both dwarfed under the plants they were carrying, "I don't usually buy tomatoes that are a metre high!" I was to learn that was how Tim did things. Not for him was the cautious approach, especially where money was concerned. We had to buy the best, even if it was only a can of salmon. Or tomato plants. My neighbours were amused and then enviously a bit cross with me when my tomatoes ripened weeks before theirs.

We acquired a cat, a lovely grey Persian, and we named her Nip, short for Catnip because she had a habit of using her teeth when she didn't get what she wanted, although I insisted her full name was really *Nepeta Cataria* because I was into Latin names for plants. She and Tim had instant rapport because he fed her bits of bacon under the table and let her 'help' him as he pottered around at work. It was fun to see them both up a ladder, Nip as close to his hands as she could get, flicking him with her paw to add to the activity in her fashion, and on one occasion I remember that they both got covered in paint. Nip was not too happy about being cleaned up after that little episode but it still didn't stop her going back to be with him every time he worked.

Meanwhile, I was attempting to get back to my work on Porsild, which by now meant putting all the research material together and writing my thesis. Son John was working for a computer company and fixed me up with a hybrid machine that I could use at home instead of having to go down to McGill and spend hours on the big computer on the campus downtown. Kim taught me a computer system called 'Multimate' that she was using at the office. It was almost out of date then, and she had no sooner taught me than she moved on to 'Word' at work and then the world went on to 'Windows', but it was all I knew so I would use this for years until my computer finally crashed.

I would disappear into my office room, converted from the boys' old bedroom, and soon be lost in papers. If Tim came into the room when I was working, he would look at me in disgust and walk out again. He spent most of his time on the telephone with his daughters, Denise on Grand Manan and Andrea in Germany, and from what I could hear a lot of the time was spent in arguments. As I had already discovered from his letters, his way of loving was to try and prevent the people he loved from making the mistakes of his past or what he conceived as the mistakes of their present. Since everyone he loved always seemed to be doing the wrong thing, he would have to lecture and shout at them until they got things right by his reasoning. Only Andrea knew how to handle him. Her German mother had had a gentle saying that went, "You are right and I have my peace." When Tim harangued his other children, there were angry fights at both ends, but when he ranted at her, usually over money, Andrea merely listened quietly until eventually he would settle down and reassure himself that she was a good girl and managing somehow quite well with the meagre allowance she had from her mother's estate and what he could spare to send her.

At the end of that first summer in Montreal, we decided to spend a month on Grand Manan. We phoned the Wilsons and booked a cabin for September. What a beautiful time it was to come back to the island, with the changing of the leaves and the clear air of fall. For the first time I found myself looking at it with different eyes: It was not 'my' island, claimed from my happily innocent tourist days, but Tim's island, or at least how he saw it. He said that White Headers had always thought of it as 'the Big Island' and a truly sinful place. Grand Manan was sinful? All these lovely friendly people I had met all the times I had been there? Surely not.

Yet there was no doubt that what had happened to Tim's poor old house on the Thoroughfare was sinful. We knew that much of it was due to neglect while Tim was in Germany, including a foundation sadly in need of repair, but the worst things that had happened to the house were not part of a natural process of decline. He told me that before he left to go home on his last visit, he had picked up two nice Australian girls hitchhiking to the Anchorage where they were camping. They told him it was cold and he suggested that they move their gear into his old house and camp inside where they would be warmer. He saw them one more time after they had moved in. They said it was 'spooky' but they were okay. Apparently, it was not long before two boys moved in with the girls and then more young people and then the real problems started with the house.

We were to hear many Grand Manan theories about who was to blame for what had been done to it on purpose, with the preference being to lay blame on itinerant workers at the Ingalls Head plant who had moved in when the girls left, or when it had got so bad that it became a 'party house', but when we went over to have a look we could hardly believe what we were seeing. The verandah had been taken off completely and chopped up for firewood on the kitchen floor, leaving marks in the boards from the cutting axe. All the windows had been smashed and the outside door was swinging in the wind. Without the steps and the verandah, it was quite a climb to get inside. We walked gingerly around on broken glass on the floor in every room. Dirty peeling wallpaper reeled off the walls, ceilings sagged, doors were gone or stood open and could not be closed, swallows nests tucked themselves into corners, railings had been wrenched off the staircase, 2x4s had been punched through the walls, and a mattress hung halfway down through a hole in the upstairs ceiling. Tim went up to the attic and found only rafters. "They took all the wood from the floor up there," he said. The well and plumbing had been vandalized.

When did I get struck by insanity? We were standing in the living room bay window looking out towards the brook. We could hear sparrows quarrelling in an overhead nest and a feather came through a crack in the ceiling and floated down to our feet. The sun was shining into the room and outside the brook was running with high tide. Fall goldenrods were blooming near the willow tree. Something in the feel of what had been this lovely old house spoke to me. Images of spending quiet summers here and cozy winters in my house in Pointe Claire seduced me. So it was here that I asked the fateful question. "Do you think," I asked Tim, "Do you think that we could fix this place up?"

We were in our cabin later that evening when an expensive car pulled up to the door. A tall, interesting-looking man, with a face carved out of privilege and power, came to call on Tim. He wasted no time with preliminaries. "I want to buy your house on the Thoroughfare," he said, taking $15,000 in cash out of his pocket and throwing it down on the table. "Take it or leave it." Tim looked at me and smiled, the consummate gambler's smile. It wasn't the money that mattered, it was the power that winning gave him. "This crazy woman wants to fix it up," he said. "Well, as you like, but if you change your mind you know where to find me," the man nodded. "Wow," I said after he left. "Who was THAT?" Tim did not tell me his name. "That was one of our island millionaires," he said, and I could see then that he had been tempted by the money but was savouring a victory that tasted sweet. "He owns property everywhere. He doesn't usually take no for an answer." Years later, Glenn McLaughlin stopped me in Grand Harbour. "I'm glad you wanted to fix up that house," he said. "I would have just torn it down."

We were consumed by excited plans for the rest of that September. As usual, because the task of fixing up this old wreck of a house was obviously almost impossible, Tim was totally enthusiastic. "Three weeks," he said unrealistically, and I was inexperienced enough to almost believe him, "you'll see, in three weeks I'll have this place liveable."

The first task was to make it secure from further damage. We went over to see Brian and Sue, who were building a big house on the Dock Road in the middle of the island, and Brian and Tim had long carpentry talks while Sue and I went picking blackberries or I watched her spreading dulse to dry as she had once done on the helicopter pad on Machias Seal. Wood was ordered and sawn and hammered into large shutters for the windows and doors. Brian climbed up on a ladder and bandaged the outer walls that once been covered by verandah roofs. When the old house looked tighter and snugger, we stood back and looked at it with approval. "See you in spring," we said, and got ready for the long drive home.

Back in Montreal that winter, we had a wonderful event to celebrate. In November, John and Kim had a new addition to the family when Michèle Hannah Dathan was born. As my first grandchild, she was, of course, the most beautiful baby in the world. Tim and I looked after her one night when her parents were going out to a party. We put her in her carry-cot in the little front room and checked often to see that she was all right before going to bed. John had given us one of those microphone systems so we could hear every sound from the other room. The trouble was that I kept hearing her and getting up to check on her all night, only to find her fast asleep. It was only when morning came that we learned why we had been disturbed. We woke to a baby crying and a man's voice talking to her, and I rushed to Michèle to see what on earth was happening with a strange man in the house. She was still peacefully sleeping, and there was no man in sight. Meanwhile, our neighbour kept on talking to his baby in the house across the road, picked up by the microphone in Michèle's room!

I was hard at work on my thesis, following the Porsild brothers to Alaska and the Mackenzie River Delta and Great Bear Lake, following the reindeer over the Brooks Range on their long trek to Reindeer Station, following the ins and outs of official acts behind the scenes. It was fascinating but I had a deadline. It all had to be completed by spring, before we started work in earnest on the old house. I certainly couldn't look for support from Tim. He hated what I was doing. "Why do you have to do all this stuff with numbers – footnotes, you call it – why do you have to keep quoting other people?" "Tim, when you write something like this, you have to work responsibly and be careful to let readers know your sources." "Well, why don't you just dash something off in your own words and never mind other people's ideas?" he asked. "Tim, you can't do that with a biography!" I laughed. "I can't just make up facts about Porsild and write them as if they're true!"

He just shook his head and went back to things he understood, which meant calling all his children to tell them what he was thinking of doing to the old house and making sure that none of them wanted it before we started work. With their approval, we went looking for a small trailer to live in before the house was usable. When we found one, he had to go out looking for a car that was large enough to tow it. The car he found, of course, was secondhand and unreliable like all the cars he would buy in the next few years, all prone to breaking down in unforeseen places. The road between Montreal and Grand Manan is now littered with memories of "this is where this or that car refused to go any further/had to be towed/pushed/abandoned" all because Tim was always sure he could always fix everything.

As spring approached, we had a call from his daughter Denise on Grand Manan. "I had to call the Fire Department, Dad," she said. "They were going to burn down your house because they think its unsafe. They were going to do it for practise." "Didn't they see that we had boarded it up?" Tim asked angrily. "Has anyone taken down the boards?" She reassured him that it was still as we had left it and she had talked to the Fire Department and they were not going to do anything like burn it down before we got there, but there was no doubt that the pressure was on for us to get back to the island quickly. Once again, unfortunately, there would not be time to finish my thesis. I hated to disappoint my professor but I had to tell Ludger that I would work on it again the next winter and hopefully finish it then.

Because we were going to be away that summer, we advertised my house for rent furnished. I was not at all happy with the response from a couple who came with a large young son and said they needed a place for a few weeks because they had had a fire in their own house. "We have a swimming pool so we'll be over at our place most of the time," the woman said, but there was something about her aggressiveness that made me uneasy. However, Tim was so anxious for us to leave as soon as possible that I said they could have it, hoping that they would only be there such a short time that surely they could not do too much damage.

The drive down east was nothing less than a nightmare. We had Nip with us in the trailer and every time we let her out we worried that she might not come back. Tim was concerned about the hitch he had rigged up, unsure whether it was the right size but it was all he had been able to obtain, and then there was always the worry as to whether the car was big or heavy enough to cope with hauling the heavy trailer behind it. It was not too bad as we followed the flat plain route to Quebec City and along the shore to Saint Jean Port Joli, spending a night in a garage parking lot beside a field of snow-white Snow Geese, nor was it too worrying along the smooth whaleback of the Trans Canada Highway above the St. Lawrence River driving towards Rivière de Loup, but when we turned south for New Brunswick, the road was even more mountainous than we had remembered and every hill became a labour of anxiety as to whether the old car would make it. No one was more relieved than we were when we finally reached the island still in one piece.

Tim parked the trailer beside the running brook and greening willow tree. For a one and only time, on that first morning we looked out to see a black-crowned night heron fishing from a rock right beside us. It was early May and the warblers were coming back. A kingfisher darted out of the willow branches and dove to the water, emerging with a shining fish in its beak. Sitting at the table in the trailer, I loved watching the brook change with every tide, with the fresh water flowing out in a narrow stream near the bottom of its channel at low tide, out under the outlet pipe under the road to the little bay on the other side where it curved its way onwards into the main harbour through the islands of rockweed-covered stones, then seeming to stop and come backwards as the saltwater filled the bay at high tide, reversing the brook current below us as the sea flowed steadily inside the outlet, filling the space of the banks higher and higher, covering the grasses and seaside goldenrod on the opposite lower side, and raising the water level up our bank to a few feet below where we were parked.

It was the beginning of an endless fascination with the movement of the tides in Grand Harbour, with the filling and emptying of the vast basin, up and down twice a day. How many tons of water would it take each day to fill it? And what of the life that was altered with each tide, the clams that Cyril Harvey would go out each day to dig when the season allowed, the mussels in the eelgrass or the periwinkles clinging to the rockweed, the ducks and geese that would swim and dive when the sea was high or the shorebirds that would peck at the edges when the mudflats stretched almost halfway out to Ingalls Head. From our viewpoint at the old house, I never tired of looking out at the peaceful horizontals, as the eastern sun rose in the morning and turned the west-side houses to a soft golden hue, or set in the evening in the fiery western sky that was mirrored in a harbour of flames, or the moon rose up in the dark of night and threw out a stream of silver blessings on the black seawater below. No matter how difficult it was going to be to fix up the old house, it would all be worth it for the gift of the tidal harbour that came with it.

Our first task with the house was to take down the shutters and look inside with horror at all that needed to be done. Where on earth would we start? Over the winter, the house had heaved more than ever. There was a huge gaping hole in the living room where the fireplace had fallen into the basement when the brick support beneath it had collapsed. The entire place had only remained standing due to the fact that Tim had asked a kind neighbour if he would put some bracing under the house when he was cutting wood that winter. Arthur Fleet had done such a good wharf job with his solid timbers underneath the house that it had withstood all the winter winds up the harbour, and we felt we owed it to him that he had saved it.

Our first priority now was to find someone who could build a real foundation. No one on the island would touch it. They would make a new one further back and move the house onto it, they said, but there was no way they would work under it. In fact, most Grand Mananers were of the opinion that we were crazy not to burn the whole place down and build a new house on a new foundation, and with our limited resources, and hindsight, I really think they were right. Even my mother, once we had started to work on it, would send snippy letters from Montreal saying, "Why don't you burn that old place down and come back home where you belong?" But there is no stopping the foolish when they get an insane idea into their heads. Eventually, we found a stonemason off island. Yes, Dave would come when he was ready, but we had to wait till he had time.

The next priority was to replace the broken wooden windows, windows that Tim had already replaced once before so he knew exactly where to go in Saint John to a wonderful old-fashioned factory, the kind where everything was done with personal, prideful care, and there we got replacements to match the ones that were now beyond repair. Putting them up was agony for both of us because Tim was in pain the whole time and I was not the most efficient of helpers and hated seeing his pain, but he was determined to keep going somehow. My only consolation was that he was happy doing it, and when we had finished we could get warm to some extent out of the wind. We had no electricity and therefore no lights and no heat inside until Richard Foster put up a temporary post on the house outside with two outlets for extension cords.

It was June already and one morning we woke up to find that the fog had rolled in. "Oh, how I love fog," I said happily on that first day. "It's so soft and beautiful and look how magical it looks over the harbour, drifting in and out like a cloud." Tim scowled at me and lit his perennial cigarette. The fog wrapped its arms around us, around the harbour, around the island, around the whole world, clammy and cold. The view of the harbour disappeared completely. Even with windows, the house was damp and perishing. At the end of the third week I snapped, "I feel as if I'm growing moss on the north side. I'll be glad when I see sun again." I was learning.

There was nothing now to do but wait for Dave. We tried phoning him but there was no answer. Tim wouldn't let me do anything until he arrived. "No use," he said morosely. "If we don't have a foundation, we don't have anything."

Starting from the Bottom

All that foggy month we waited, with no news from the mainland. Meanwhile, Tim decided that the little trailer was too confining to live in for long, so we moved over into the house. On our first night upstairs, I had a nightmare that the attic and then the house was over-run with rats, and they were scuttling all around me, with skinny tails reminding me of snakes, and looking at me with evil eyes. I woke up screaming my head off. I also lay in bed and worried that the house would collapse while we were in it, especially on the night after I had been cleaning in the hall and heard a terrible sound that I thought was the roof coming down. Running out of the house in panic, I found bricks from the fallen chimney scattered all over the brook-side grass.

On the magic sunny morning of July 1, without warning, the yard was suddenly full of trucks. Dave and his crew had finally arrived and it was a joyous day as the men started to work at last. The plan was to remove the crumbling foundation one wall at a time, leaving the house still supported on Arthur's magnificent poles, and slowly build up new walls with concrete blocks. They would do one wall and then leave it for a week or so before coming back to do the next, and by the end of summer we would have a good foundation. How I wish we had asked them to do the basement floor while it was all open and they had their concrete mixer! The floor had been concreted originally, but it had heaved while exposed to the elements and only part of it remained whole while the rest allowed water to come up through the ground. Tim thought there had never been a flooding problem down there and I was still seeing the house as a summer place where it might not matter, so many decisions were made that I would later regret. With the much-too-late and therefore useless wisdom of hindsight I can say it - it would have been so easy for them to do it then!

The other part of the plan was that all the men would stay in the house while they were on island. They had brought camp cots so the five of them could sleep dormitory style in the front bedroom. To have a working toilet of sorts, Tim and I had to go down to the brook for flushable water, carrying a large container that was very heavy when full as we struggled to bring it back up the bank, across to the house, and up the stairs. This had not been too much of a problem when only Tim and I were in the house, but with the addition of all these people we had to do this more often. Although Tim was in constant pain, he was too proud to ask for their help and insisted that I was to say nothing, so we just made our trips as best we could. There was no working basin or shower in the bathroom because the well had been rendered useless. Calls to various people about cleaning out the well had resulted in refusals, and the off-island well-driller, who said he would do it or give us a new one, never appeared. We boiled a kettle and did dab washes as we could.

For drinking and cooking water, we bought a new garbage can and went up to Denise's, where we could also bathe or shower and wash our clothes. Coming back with the full can in the trunk of the car, I found I resented every bump that spilled our precious load. With five men and ourselves to feed, I had only an electric kettle, frying pan and large pot for cooking vegetables. This was interesting on the days when the men needed both the outside electric outlets for their work, yet I was expected to have a cooked meal ready for them as soon as they were ready for their dinner. I have never been more reminded of the difficulties of life in a refugee camp with more passion that I did that summer. Living without running water in a dirty house that was no more that an old construction camp, always somehow feeling dirty, and resenting furiously how much water it took just to cook a few potatoes, how did people isolated in terrible places like the Gaza Strip manage with no water and no hope that life would ever get better?

Dave and his men began by knocking down and pulling out the east foundation wall, which was already collapsing so came out easily. "They used salt water in that old cement between the stones," someone told me knowingly. "That's why its falling apart now." By now a parking lot of island trucks had joined the others in the driveway, bringing onlookers and advisers and sceptics alike. Arthur was there with other neighbours to supervise, and over and again we complimented him on his solid basement supports. A tour bus actually stopped to show the tourists the extraordinary sight, reminding me of being on a similar bus in New York City when the driver stopped to show us the sad drunks in the Bowery. "Get your cameras out, folks!" I can still hear him say while I tried not to look at pitiful human degradation. Why do people do that? It's like stopping to see an accident with no intention of being able to help, just to look at mangled car and human bodies. Well, I suppose our activity site was something interesting to look at, but imagining all the wiseacre comments inside the bus made me turn away in embarrassment.

A limousine with blue-tinted windows pulled up at the side of the road. When the rear window came down, a head with blue-tinted hair looked out. "What are they doing to that house?" the lady asked imperiously. Very conscious of my overall dirtiness and shabbiness, I tried to remove myself one step from the scene. "I think they are trying to fix it up," I said. "Oh," she said dismissively. She turned her head to the shore and waved in the direction of Cheney Island. "We used to own all that," she said, "except for some riff-raff that had a few shacks at the White Head end." It did not seem like a good idea to tell her that one of the riff-raff was fixing up the house. She admired our huge saltspray rose bush, magnificent in full bloom in the middle of all the trucks, wheelbarrows, concrete mixer, concrete blocks, sand, wood, and rubbish, and I asked her if she would like some for her hotel room. "Thank you," she said when I gave them to her. The blue window went up again, the limo glided off to the corner before turning up the road to North Head, and I stood looking longingly after them. Once upon a time, a long time ago it now seemed, I, too, had been clean and dressed nicely and had ridden in taxis in my city of Montreal. Would the day ever come when I would be clean and do that again?

Actually, I did have to go up to Montreal very soon. The tenants in my house in Pointe Claire would be moving out any day and I needed to check it after they left, also all this work on the Thoroughfare house meant that we needed to borrow some money. The island bank, knowing only too well the state of the house and our limited resources, turned us down flat, so we had to look elsewhere for help. It was decided I would go up alone and see what I could negotiate with my bank at home.

On the ferry going over to the mainland, I sat and talked to Annie Foote. Annie had been one of our first visitors as soon as we moved into the house. She had come bearing a wooden plant stand that she said had been removed from the house when it was empty and now she was bringing it back. She hoped other people would follow her example. Now she said that she was on her way to Vancouver by bus, going out to see her son, so I told her that I was driving as far as Montreal and would she like to come with me and I could take her to the bus station there? Annie and I had a great trip to Montreal. All the way over the mountains of Maine and through the green valleys and fields of the Eastern Townships, she told me her wonderful stories of Wood Island, the little out-island where Preston and Pearla had also grown up on the south side of Grand Manan, stories so warm and thick with detail that I felt I had been cosily wrapped in a tightly-knit shawl. Annie's delivery was long and slow, and she took a long time to get to the point, but we had plenty of time on our side. There were family stories and ghost stories – who could forget the ghost on Wood Island seen by her little niece, when the hair went up on the back of Annie's neck when the child said she had seen him walking through the closed door? - and fun stories where right triumphed over wrong with just the right dose of irony. We spent that night in my mother's Montreal apartment after I called and asked if she could put up two strays instead of one, and I wondered what those two made of each other, each so different in every way and each so sure of the rightness of where they were coming from, but we arrived late at night and left early in the morning so there was not much time for them to make comparisons.

My old Royal Bank in Pointe Claire was now being run entirely by women. The loan manager listened to me carefully when I showed her the pictures of the house, making no bones about its sad condition, and told her what we were trying to do. I asked for only $15,000, because that was something we felt we could reasonably repay, and she agreed to give me the loan without hesitation because, she said, "I believe in you." When I walked out of there I was floating. Later, we were able to get a larger mortgage from the Royal Bank in Saint John, based on her initial truly blind faith which I have never forgotten. I went back at the end of that summer to show her photographs of what we had done to justify her generous belief.

There was little joy in what I found in my little bungalow, however. In the brief few weeks that they occupied it, my tenants had treated the house roughly, leaving the kitchen stove looking like it was ready to be baked as a pizza with spills from tomato sauce all down it. There were white marks on all the living room furniture from cold drinks set down without a coaster. The grass had not been cut and the whole back garden beds had been trampled down. "It was that boy," my neighbours said in disgust. "He just walked all the way down on top of them, crushing the flowers for fun." It turned out that he was the one who had caused their home fire, playing with matches, so I suppose it was lucky that he didn't decide to play with matches for fun at my house.

Back on Grand Manan, I could see that Dave and crew had completed the second foundation wall on the north side. That was the side where I now had an unwanted vegetable garden. Tim had mistaken my enthusiasm for what I visualized as a pretty English flower garden as wanting a more typical Grand Manan one, so he again asked Arthur when he was roto-tilling his yard if he would do the same for me. Both of them were so proud of what they had created for me, a fifteen by thirty foot bed "in the same place that Owen had his vegetables," Arthur said, referring to the original owner. Trying to show I was as keen as they were, I turned over a few perennial weeds, thinking they would be like my annual weeds at home and just nourish the earth as they rotted. Arthur soon put me right on that. "Every one of those bits of roots will be another weed," he said. "You'd best be pulling them right out."

Since I had no choice, I did as I was told, and my 'pretty little garden' became a splendid place for growing peas and beans, lettuce, Swiss chard, beetroots, and carrots, all of which Tim wouldn't eat. At least everyone coming up the island, driving straight towards the brook and the house before they turned the corner to go north towards North Head, would see that there were people in the disgraceful old house who were serious about fixing it up and staying because they were making a garden now, weren't they? And I was very proud of my produce, although I didn't have a clue what I was doing and happily gave away radishes the size of my fist because I thought that was just because the soil was so good here on the island. What I didn't grow was blue potatoes, which someone, maybe it was Otis Green, gave me when he brought back the coloured windows that Denise had given him from the house. "Blue potatoes!" I exclaimed, and as the cooking water ran a deep blue and we ate the flesh that turned a sort of grey, I learned that was the origin of the term Bluenose for the people of Nova Scotia who had grown and eaten them in the past.

The big day came when Vernon Parker and his dad put in real electricity. As feared, they found a deserted rat's nest in the hall ceiling, which they cleaned out while doing the wiring. The whole place of course had to be re-wired and I love looking at the results of the work that they did for us that day. Not only was it heavenly then to have light and heat at last, but, from that day forward, every switch and light socket in every room in the house is somehow crooked from when it was mounted on those far from straight inside walls.

Dave decided that he would do both of the last two foundation walls at the same time, and called in Wade Dakin and his big machinery to dig a deep moat down to the level of the basement floor on the brook and road sides. These happened to be the only sides of the house with entry doors, so, to give us access, that night before we went to bed Tim fashioned a rickety contraption with a ladder and two of the shutters he had made before we left in the fall. In the morning I heard a noise downstairs and went down to investigate.

When I opened the door on the brook side, Annie and her brother Bernard Lorimer were standing on the makeshift drawbridge, each holding a chair. "We've brought you some furniture," Annie said, handing me one and passing the other forward from Bernard. They were heading back down for more when I heard Annie say "Bernard, don't fall" followed immediately by "Bernard, I said, don't fall." Bernard was already in the moat, but fortunately he was relatively unhurt. While he continued to stand there, they passed me two more chairs and then came a round table that they rolled up the slope and I rolled into the hall. Finally, I helped them both inside. "Well, I'm here," Annie said in her most sepulchral tone of voice, "and I may never leave again." Tim made his drawbridge a little more secure while I made them tea.

We still had the drawbridge when we saw an ad in the paper for a secondhand fridge, owned by the American minister and his sweet crippled wife at the end of Bancroft Point. "I suppose you'll send someone with a truck to collect it?" they asked when we decided to take it. Tim shook his head. Being a small man, he had long ago learned the secret of leverage. To their and my amazement, while we sat and talked he used a plank of wood to lever and move that big heavy fridge out of their cottage and into the trunk of our car. With one half inside and the other sticking out, the car groaning from the weight, we drove back to the Thoroughfare and I laughed all the way home. "Tim, you are incredible!" I said. "Will you ask Brian to help you get it into the house?" He would have none of it, so all alone he moved that big thing up and over the step and into the kitchen.

With the new table and chairs set up in the wallpaper-peeling dining room, the once beautiful floor covered in tar, we had visitors from Montreal for supper one evening. We were just finishing dessert by candlelight, laughing and joking about old times and our present life in the middle of a construction site, when we suddenly looked up and saw two strangers standing in the doorway. They had come up the drawbridge in the dark and come inside when we didn't hear them and followed the light and laughter until they found us. "Would you like to buy a grand piano?" they asked. It was Joyce and Russell Upton from the big house they were restoring in North Head and they had one of those old square pianos that take up so much space and are so difficult to tune. "Could we?" I asked Tim, but of course we couldn't. I think Audrey Ingalls acquired it eventually and it went to St. Paul's Anglican Hall.

We had a lot of visitors that summer. Andrea came from Germany with a delightful boyfriend with whom we all fell in love. Big tall Karsten had a ready smile for everyone. Tim's two older daughters, Darlene and Shirley, came from Halifax and Boston at the same time and, together with Denise and Brian on island, they had a big Cossaboom reunion where they all posed in the crazy gaudy shorts that Darlene had made for them. Karsten and Andrea, when they weren't in the trailer, took Tim's big old car and went around the Cabot Trail, not without adventures when it misbehaved.

My old naturalist friend, Ralph Hoskins, turned up unexpectedly one day. Dear Ralph, who was already unsteady with the onset of Parkinsons, had left his car the other side, got off the ferry in North Head, and had started walking down the road when someone picked him up and brought him down to see us. He came, I know, because he was worried about me, and about what I had got myself into with the old house. He was not reassured when he saw it. Everything I showed him with excitement only made the worry creases in his face get deeper. Tim and I both tried to make him feel better but I don't think it worked. He was such a cautious, guarded person, who liked his life to be orderly and carefully planned, and our whole venture was much too uncomfortable and terrifyingly uncertain for him, not to mention all the hard labour involved. I took him back to North Head and put him on the ferry with mixed feelings, glad to have seen him and grateful for his concern, but I felt this was probably the last time I would see him on the island and he would be going home still worrying about me. "See you in Montreal next winter," I said as cheerfully as I could. "Take care of yourself, old friend."

We had another visitor early that summer who was a friend of my old buddy Ben Lapin, the Montreal Field Naturalist who had led the trip to see the Snow Geese at Cap Tourmente and told Gail Pflaster to look me up when she came to Grand Manan. Ben was another one who had come to the Anchorage Inn in the early nineteen sixties, and was proud of his friendship with Gleason Green, especially after the article about Gleason called 'My Most Unforgettable Character' in *Readers Digest.* On that visit, he had come over from Eastport on the *Grand Manan III* with a bunch of birders. They were on the deck looking at a flock of phalaropes swimming below when a woman came up to him and said loudly "Say, is it true that those birds can walk on water?" Ben was Jewish and the Anglican minister was standing near by. "You'd better ask the man with his collar on backwards," he replied. "He knows a lot more about that sort of thing than I do."

Ben had once given a talk in the Redpath Museum for the Montreal Field Naturalists. The talk was on 'Astronomy in Ninety Minutes?' It was a bit daunting to know that we were in for a data-stuffed talk that would last at least an hour and a half, but I went with Ralph and together we climbed up the steps at the back of one of those old lecture halls where the listeners sit on three sides looking down on the speaker at ground floor. It was terribly hot in that room that night, and dear old Ben went on and on and on. Suddenly, I became aware that my very proper friend Ralph, who never did anything improper, was nudging me improperly in the thigh. "Oh dear," I whispered, "I fell asleep. Did I snore?" Ever the gentleman, Ralph said politely "You were breathing rather heavily." Well, we all know about my reputation for snoring loudly. When Ben's long talk was finally over, I went down to ground level and found my friend Isabelle where she was sitting near the door. "Oh, didn't he go on forever," I complained gently, "and my, wasn't it hot in there. I fell asleep." "I know," said Isabelle, equally gently, and I realized with horror why Ralph had had to take desperate measures to wake me when the whole room knew I was not exactly listening to the speaker. I am always terrified of falling asleep in church or meetings!

When Gail arrived on the Thoroughfare, she had just been to Susan Wilcox for a pedicure. She showed us her polished toenails and beautiful feet clad in her elegant sandals and we tried not to show her too much of our awful house. "What are we going to do with her when she gets here?" Tim had asked, ever the conscientious host. We decided we'd take her out in our rowboat to the Ross Island Lighthouse. Gingerly, Gail climbed inside but we were no sooner out of the bay when she cried out in panic for Tim not to go out over the deep water but to stick closer to the shallows at the side of the harbour. The longer trip was hard for Tim but he did as he was told. We explored the old lighthouse that was already in ruins and Tim looked for the coin that he felt should have been placed over a door for good luck.

Because we had taken so long to get out there, when it came time to leave, the tide was running out. By the time we reached Romig's point, the mudflats were emerging and we could go no further. There was nothing we could do but tie the boat to the highest rock and make our way on foot through the mud to the shore. Gail held her sandals up high as she squished her way through the oozing muck. "Ugh," she said, "Ugh, this is horrible!" "You've had a pedicure and now you're having a mud bath," we laughed, trying to cheer her up. "Think how beautifully soft your feet are going to be." It was an awful way to treat a guest but we really had no choice. Gail went straight back to Susan for another pedicure, but she was good enough not to hold it against us because she has come every year since then to visit and check on the progress of the house. I, meanwhile, had the joy of going back to get the boat later that day, of floating in with the rising tide and watching the eelgrass rolling below me like underwater tumbleweed until tying up by the bank inside the brook.

John and Kim and the baby came in August. Michèle was now nine months old and had begun to crawl so there was no way they could stay in the dirty old house. We rented an apartment from Joyce and Ron Benson in Seal Cove so we could holiday together and I must say it was wonderful to have a clean place to stay for just a little while as well as enjoying having my family with us. Michèle was a born mimic. If we said the name 'Tim', she crinkled up her eyes exactly as he did. She had such a sunny nature and we had so much fun with her. The difficulties of our life on Grand Manan were too much for Kim, however. She was an efficient girl who liked to get everything done in sensible, reasonable time. Back at the old house, we were still waiting for the well man to arrive. One day I saw his trucks and chased them but he only sped away and took off back on the ferry. Kim was furious. "I couldn't live here," she said. "All this waiting around for people who never come. I couldn't stand it!" "It's not so easy on an island," we told her, and perhaps also to tell ourselves after all the frustrations we had had waiting, "it's not like the city where there are plenty of people to do the job. Here there are only a few people and we all have to take our turn."

They had gone back to Montreal when the well driller suddenly arrived out of nowhere, just as Dave and his men had come the first time. One minute, there was nothing but a peaceful driveway and the green field looking out towards Betty's house next door, and suddenly there were trucks and men and a giant house-high drill in the yard and they were telling us they were going to drill a new well. "Couldn't you just clean out the old one?" we asked but they shook their heads. It was too close to the 'green' new concrete and they were afraid it would cave in the wall.

So they drilled a new well. When they got down to eighty feet, the level of the last one, there was water there and Tim begged them to stop, but they decided there was not enough flow and drilled deeper. When the water flowed to their satisfaction at a hundred to a hundred and twenty feet down, they topped it off, took their money, and the whole noisy scene evaporated in seconds, leaving us with water that was never as good as the water in the house before. "They should have stopped at that earlier level," Tim fumed. "I told them but of course they knew better. That was when they hit the ledge with the good water. Below that, they got down to the good old Grand Harbour iron and manganese and now we'll have stinky rusty water forever."

Unfortunately, he was right. It has taken years of trying to filter out the bad to obtain something usable, years of brown 'whites' in the laundry, years of buying bottled water for drinking and cooking, until I invested my life's savings in an expensive system that I hope will finally cure the curse of that Grand Harbour water. Forever, I pray.

Looking Back and Moving Forwards

We had many Grand Manan visitors that first summer, but it was from Helen Ingalls and Janice Naves that I began to learn something of the history of the old house. They came in apologetically, trying to be polite about what we were doing, but obviously shocked at what had happened to a place that had once been a beloved part of their family. It seems that it was built in 1902 by Abram Dakin, whose occupation was listed in the genealogical records as 'sail-maker' but I have no doubt that he did other things as well. We were told that he worked out at Dark Harbour one winter for Isaac Newton, one of Grand Manan's most important men in that period, and when the time came for him to be paid, he had earned something in the nature of $1700 or $1800. "That's too much money for a poor man to have," the old man had scowled at him. That was the money that enabled Abram to build his new house, a good house and a big one, just down the road in Grand Harbour from where Isaac Newton had a splendid mansion in what is sometimes known locally as 'Millionaires Row'.

Abram and his Prince Edward Island wife, Caroline, had a large family even before the new house was built. They had lost one little girl because of a tragic fire in their first small home, a not unusual sad happening in the days when children took candles to light their rooms when they went to bed. Like so many other Grand Mananers, they may also have lost more children in the plagues that hit the island in the late 1800s, when grief-stricken parents might be burying one child in the cemetery and come home to find another one dead, as island historian Gleneta Hettrick once told me.

The Dakins' first house was attached to the larger one originally, which explained a strange door to the east of our house that seemed to go nowhere. The little building had been removed and placed further up the Thoroughfare on the harbour side, and was now the house where Jenny Wilson's brother and his wife lived. The only time I saw inside that house was years later when I was asked to collect for the Heart and Stroke Foundation and Bessie asked me in for a cup of coffee. There was a wonderful smell of bread baking in the kitchen as we sat there, and she told me that her daughter had given her a new bread-maker that she was trying out. Suddenly, there was not such a wonderful smell and she rushed over to the machine, and all hell broke loose as she called for her husband in the other room. When she lifted the lid, she could see that the bread had risen up and was overflowing everywhere and it was the worst mess you could ever imagine. Apparently, Bessie thought the little loaves that the machine was supposed to bake were too small, so she had doubled the recipe. I thought it was a good time for me to get out of there!

Helen remembered that there was a huge portrait of Queen Victoria in her grandparents' home. "They used to sit in the hall around the wood stove," she said. "That way they could look out the window at the main road and see who was travelling along it. They never used the living room. That was for laying out the body before a funeral." It had, however, been used for at least one wedding reception, because Helen and Hayward had had theirs there. "It used to seem so much larger," she said in surprise. "The whole house was decorated with water lilies and it was lovely."

When the old folks had passed away and the younger Dakin family dispersed, there were only two unmarried siblings left at home. Owen had a large barn at the back and kept horses that he needed to meet the boat and transport people around. Some of the travelling salesmen used to stay in the house while they were doing business on the island, and someone remembered carpets being spread out in the living room for display purposes. Everyone remembers Owen's sister Sarah as Aunt Sed. She had a crippled hand and she used to sit in a rocking chair by the kitchen window where she, too, could watch the world go by. Countless adults now nearly as old as I am, or older, have told me how Aunt Sed welcomed all the children and they would be allowed to go up to the attic and play with old clothes and musical instruments and even sleep on the floor up there. After Aunt Sed died, bachelor Owen was married for the first time. "You'll be dead in a year," one of his friends warned him, but he went ahead and got married anyway. He wed a widow, who was Jenny Wilson's mother Violet Avery, and unfortunately the prophecy was fulfilled.

Jenny and Eldred came to see us one evening, and we all stood outside and looked across the harbour to see if we could see the cabins where we had stayed with them on Ingalls Head Road. We couldn't see very much, but we could see a light shining from the little lighthouse that Eldred had put up by Sisters Beach. Jenny remembered coming to help her mother clean the old house on the Thoroughfare when she was married to Owen. "They slept downstairs," she said, "and they took out the back stairs into the kitchen and made a toilet there. And I fell down into it," she added with a laugh. The temporary ceiling had not held when she walked out onto it upstairs and she had come right through to ground level.

She pointed out the spot by the kitchen door where Owen had had a sink to wash his hands when he came in from working outside in his garden. The floor had been damaged by the water and the walls were coming apart because we had done little inside work until the foundation was finished. "So many people do it the wrong way round," Dave had told us, "they fix all the walls and then everything cracks and they have to do it all over again." Eldred took a piece of loose plaster in his hand, the old plaster and horsehair with laths behind it, and smiled. "I used to love to eat that stuff when I was a kid," he said.

Tim had bought the house originally for his first wife and their children, so the bedrooms upstairs had a later history for us. The big bedroom was Brian's room, the middle one Liege's, the purple one at the back belonged to Denise, and the little one at the front with windows on two sides was the domain of Darlene, Shirley having gone to live with her grandmother in Boston. Perhaps it was Shirley's potential bedroom, the only room left at the front of the house, that was turned into a bathroom in Ruth's time. The east window in Darlene's room looked down on the housed entryway into the cellar, and I learned that the Cossaboom youngsters used its roof to escape without being seen when they were off on disapproved adventures. Tim said the house was full of young people during Ruth's time, and of course he disapproved very much of their parties, but for many younger Grand Mananers the house would always be 'the Cossaboom house' dating back to those hospitable times.

When we started to work on the house, one of the young folks who had come to the parties in that period offered to help us fix it up, but I doubt if he remembered his offer later and we certainly didn't need it at the time. It was late in the evening and we were about to go to bed when this nice young man appeared at the door. We had seen him around the island and he had always been polite and friendly and helpful, but he was very much the worse for wear that night. He could barely stand and he was completely and utterly sloshed. "Jush come to tell you, Tim," he said generously, with a smile as wide as tomorrow, "not to worry about fix-shing up thish housh. We'll get all the boysh together and we'll fixsh it up for you in no time!" Tim gave me a look that I interpreted as a warning that this is what happened to people like me when we drank alcohol and I returned his look with one that said I think it's a good time for me to go to bed and let you deal with this yourself. As I said, I doubt if this expansive offer was remembered the next morning.

After Ruth and the children had moved up to North Head, Tim had come back to live in the house briefly with his mother. Blanche Cossaboom had been in the nursing home but had been somewhat of 'a challenge' so they had called Ruth to take her home. Ruth had tried but it was not easy, and eventually she called Tim in Germany and told him that he had to come and look after her himself. He installed her in a hospital bed in the little room off the kitchen, where Owen and Violet had once slept, when Crystal came over from Germany for a visit in February and was with them during the Groundhog Gale.

When the terrible storm hit the island, Tim was at the Legion, up the road past Isaac Newton's house and opposite the Newton Store. He had just written an exam to pass his Captain's papers and had to come home at the height of the gale. The wind up the harbour was so strong that he said he almost had to crawl home. When he got to the house, he had to fight with the door to open it and then fight again to close it against the wind. Safe in the kitchen at last, he turned to shout, panting, "Is everyone all right? Are you all right, Crystal?" Crystal was coming through from the pantry with a tea tray for herself and his mother. Serene as always, she looked surprised. "Of course," she said. Tim went off into drama. "Haven't you looked out the window?" he demanded. "Haven't you seen the sheds floating, smashed up on the shore, haven't you seen the waves, haven't you seen...." "I thought it was just a normal winter's day in Canada," Crystal said. How I wish I had met that wonderful woman!

By now I was getting to meet quite a few Grand Mananers, some of whom had never even talked to a tourist and perhaps didn't care if they ever met one. It has always bothered me to hear tourists or newcomers talking patronisingly about the islanders. "Grand Mananers this" or "Grand Mananers that," they say, as if they are talking about a colony of puffins that all do exactly the same. I think it was after one of these irritating conversations that Bessie Bass said wisely, "No one should say anything about the island until they have lived here for at least ten years." It is true that in many ways islanders think and act alike because they have spent all their years together, but I soon found that they were like people everywhere, they were all kinds, and most of them, even the scamps, likeably so. "If you like us, we'll like you," Muriel Cheney once told me on the ferry, and I did. That included the boys down the road from the old house who were getting into trouble elsewhere but were good boys when they were with us. Tim liked to teach them how to play chess or talk to them about stamp collecting and they liked to have someone who would take them seriously and just talk to them as well as feed them cookies and cola. I liked having them because of once having my sons and their friends around my house at home. One of the boys was Henry, who kindly bought me matches for the fireplace when he went away on a trip, big matches in a round red carton marked 'Dynamite', and I have them still to remind me of how he helped me in the garden.

Although I was learning to love a great many of the people I met, there was still an unspoken barrier between us. My 'from away' label could never be hidden, because I was out of the circle of understanding and familiarity that enclosed the insiders. It reminded me of being on the bus with those lovely young students from the Wildlife Resources Department at Macdonald College when we were adventuring together so long ago. If I mentioned something from the past, one of them would say, "Twenty years ago? I wasn't even born!" so I realized then that there was no way that we could share a past and I had to settle for the present. In the same way, there was no way that I could share a remembering of a Grand Manan past, but at least I could learn what they could tell me about it and join with everybody to share the present with all its joys and sorrows.

Not since I was a child in Guyana had I lived in a community that was so close in sharing all the events of the present. We all went to the post office for our mail, so in Grand Harbour we got all the Grand Harbour news that filtered down eventually to include all the island news from the other post offices in Seal Cove and North Head. Not that we always got the news right. It has often been said that if someone hurt his finger in North Head, by the time the news got down to Seal Cove, it was reliably reported that he was having his leg amputated, so we always had to take our news with a grain of scepticism.

But it was in the important things that the community became one. When the ambulance or the fire engine went up or down the road, we all stopped what we were doing and listened. Who was in trouble now? Back in Montreal, the sirens went up and down the streets and the highways all the time and we never listened because whatever the trouble might be it was always to do with someone else, someone we didn't know, but here it might be – well, count the houses as the ambulance went down – no, not there, or there, or there, not down Ingalls Head, so it must be further down, Seal Cove maybe – well, someone would tell us later. And, collectively, Grand Mananers stand together when times are tough or when things go wrong, and no community is more generous when there has been a tragedy of any kind.

I met a great number of young people when we went up to Denise's before we got water in the house. Denise was baby-sitting and the children were everywhere when we got there, and the parents would pop in to drop them off or pick them up. One of her friends amused me greatly when she told me how she loved to hunt in the fall. When she drove her fisherman husband down to the wharf early in the morning in the hunting season, she said she didn't bother to get dressed, just put on her dressing gown and climbed into the truck, but she always had her gun at the ready in case she saw a deer on the way back. Coming from the city where no one I knew hunted (except one naturalist friend who hunted ducks until the day they shot nine beautiful wood ducks and he put down his rifle and never hunted again), I cherished a wonderful image of a small round person with bright red hair, wearing a fluffy pink dressing gown, scrambling out of her truck and racing across a field with gun in hand to shoot a deer she had seen in the distance. Of course, if she had seen one she would simply have shot it through the open window of the truck, but I liked my vision better.

She and Denise got up to all kinds of mischief together, including the night they put all the lawn ornaments they could find on the RCMP lawn. They were a naughty, flighty but thoroughly lovable pair, and Tim despaired of his daughter at every turn. When she came to the house, it was often to get money out of him for the children, and she usually got what she wanted because Denise always got what she wanted, but it was not without a row. Like her father, she was so unfailingly generous herself that it was easy to forgive her for almost anything. There is only one Denise in the world and she is predictably unpredictable, courageous, maddening, and absolutely wonderful! Stories about her alone would fill a book, but one that is typical is when she was looking after Robert Ingalls after his stroke. When she arrived at the house one morning, Audrey told her that her husband was very down and he was not talking that day. Denise promptly walked over to his bed. "Hello, Robert, how are you today?" she asked brightly. There was no answer. "Oh, he's dead!" Denise exclaimed in surprise, and pulled the sheets over his head. "You'd better call the funeral home." From under the bedclothes came a deep smothered chuckle and Robert emerged with a big grin on his face.

Summer turned into fall and at last we had a new foundation. It was an exciting day when Dave removed Arthur's posts, a fraction higher than the new replacements, and lowered the house onto the new steel supports as well as the new concrete walls. No one knew exactly what would happen when the house was lowered, and we all tried not to look worried, but there was a slight bump when I was coming down the stairs and that was all anyone felt. No walls or ceilings fell down any more than what had happened already, no one standing underneath was killed in the process, in fact it was just as if this sort of thing happened every day. To say we were delighted is putting it mildly. The house would take a while to settle completely, especially in the archway from the living room to the hall and above that, but we felt that that was to be expected. Tim was only annoyed that Dave had done something wrong with the foundation that would prove a problem later. He had put the basement windows on the south side, the side that would eventually be covered by a restored verandah. "I asked him to put them on the north side," Tim said bitterly. "Why does no one ever listen to me?"

We would have another problem with placement under the verandah when it came to getting a septic tank, but before that happened, and before Dave left for good, we had an exciting job to finish. The fireplace that had fallen out of the living room into the basement needed to be replaced. We borrowed a dory from Brian and went over to a spot on Long Island where he had seen flat green stones on the beach at low tide that would be perfect for the purpose. It was very foggy that day, I remember, and it was quite scary being out there and seeing nothing but a cotton wool world. "Do we have to ask the people who own the island if we can take away their stones?" I asked, but Tim said there was no problem with removing anything from the inter-tidal zone.

We were as proud as could be when we laid the lovely stones down on the living room floor. Dave started in the basement to rebuild the collapsed support column up to the level of the floor before he came upstairs and began to build up bricks at a neat angle inside the corner of the fireplace, joining the flue to what was left higher up inside the house. He had checked the exposed chimney where it went up through the attic, and pronounced it safe, but the part above the roof that had fallen off and frightened me earlier would have to re-built by Stephen Harvey. It was fascinating to watch as Dave added the outer fireplace and hearth, putting the stones together carefully and doing a beautiful job. Last to be put back was the original carved wooden mantelpiece that Brian had saved by taking it home to his house in case he needed it. When Dave had finished, we all stood back to admire his handiwork. Lighting a fire would have to wait for the final chimney, but meanwhile our new fireplace certainly looked 'right mighty'.

When it came to the septic tank, it seemed that we did not need to have one legally, because it was grandfathered into the ownership of the house that we could do what had always been done, which was for our toilet water to be flushed out into the brook. I was adamant that this had to be changed. "It may be all right to do it because it was done that way before," I told Tim, "but there's no way I want to look out and see our toilet paper going up and downstream with the tide."

Everett Dakin said he would be glad to install a new septic tank whenever we were ready for him. We told him we would be able to pay for this because we had applied for a provincial housing loan. Unfortunately, that meant that he had to double the price he had originally quoted because now he had to follow the rules and not just give us a septic tank but also create a large septic field. That loan created a problem that seemed to come up with everything. We now not only had an inspector coming round and telling us we had to do this or that, or we couldn't do this or that, as for example we couldn't do things like using secondhand outside doors but had to buy new expensive ones, and in addition all our services were much higher priced, so that the loan became a farce. "Doesn't anyone realize that we're still having to pay for everything?" we complained to each other but there are some things in life you can't change. Except that I would be very wary of asking for a government loan of any kind again. Are those loans really intended to help the people who need them, or are they set up as a screen that looks good on government statistics to create job employment or help businesses, I wonder, with just a hint of disappointed cynicism.

Still, since we had no choice, we told Everett to go ahead. The next problem was where to put the tank because it had to be so many feet away from both the well and the brook and there had to be at least fifty feet of drainage field. It was finally decided to put it on the brook side. Unfortunately, we were out when Everett's crew came to dig the hole. "Oh, no," we cried when we got home and rushed off to find and tell him "Everett, you can't put the septic tank there! It's not only right under the living room window but when we put back the verandah it will be inaccessible underneath!"

A new hole for the tank was dug a few feet northwards and then the tractor arrived to plough up the drainage field. By now I was pretty proud of my once unwanted vegetable garden that had produced so well all that summer. There was still a good crop of carrots to be dug when the tractor arrived, but when they had finished, Arthur's grand roto-tilling and all my hard labour, beds, carrots and everything, had disappeared under the plough. I looked out the window as the men stood there afterwards, three large Dakin men leaning on shovels and one tall thin man adding insult to outrage. He was standing there while they were talking, chewing one of my carrots they had just dug up.

Fall turned into winter all too quickly. The newly dug septic field turned from golden brown to white. When the temperature outside read zero, it was zero in the attic and pretty cold below that. It was time to go back to my other home, the one in Montreal, and turn my head back from old houses and once again think of that Porsild man and finishing my thesis. It was time to see my old naturalist friends again and to think of Christmas and little Michèle tottering around a Christmas tree with ornaments high out of her reach. When I sent out Christmas cards from Pointe Claire that December, they would show a house standing proudly above the ice-skimmed brook and snowy fields, a house that would wait patiently for us to go back to work on it when we returned to Grand Manan next spring.

Christmas Past and Present

Whenever I thought of Grand Manan and Montreal, I always imagined that I would be spending summers on the island and winters in my home in the city. I never imagined that I would not be able to go to see my mother every so often in Cote St. Luc, or see my grand-daughter as she was growing up and visit college and naturalist friends on West Island, or wave to my Pointe Claire neighbours across the fence. The trouble was that Tim was obviously unhappy away from the house on the island and this winter there was nothing for him to do while I worked frantically on finishing the Porsild thesis.

A lot of things came to an end in Montreal that winter. As it turned out, it would be the last Christmas that I would spend in the house in Pointe Claire. I am glad to remember it as a happy one, because it would also be the last winter that we would see John and Kim and Michèle together. The ending of a marriage is sometimes nearly as painful for others as it is for the people going through it, especially where children are involved, but I think John and Kim did it the gentlest way possible under the unhappy circumstances. Michèle went each day to her daycare, which gave her continuity and love, and one or other parent picked her up or delivered her there, although her main home was always with John. My granddaughter is a beautiful and lovely adult now, and I am so proud of her, but I also have to say how very proud I am of my son, who has been the most wonderful of fathers.

Denise and her boys, Ryan and Dustin, came to see us over the Christmas holidays and we took them to the top of Westmount Mountain to see the view of the city below and tried to find things to give them a good time. Then it was back to the grind for me and more of nothing to do for Tim until finally, in spring, I finished my thesis. I handed it in to Professor Ludger Müler Wille with profound relief. His relief too, I think, because I had taken so long to finish it that he had begun to wonder if I ever would. "One day, I will explain what took me so long to finish it," I said, expressing my thanks for all his support and understanding, but at the same time feeling a huge sense of freedom now that I could go back to Grand Manan unburdened by the weight of completing what I had promised for the thesis. Only the never-ending biography completion would hang on my conscience for more years than I care to confess, but for the moment that could be put to one side.

When we left that May, the Pointe Claire house was rented furnished to Expo baseball player Vance Law and his family, which gave the neighbourhood children a great thrill. Later, a team of wonderful men took it over for a number of months. They were working on the computer designs for the Canadian Navy frigates being built in Saint John. All of these people treated the house carefully, perhaps because they had houses of their own elsewhere, and one of the men even left a nice note to say how much they had enjoyed living there. It was only after we decided to rent the house unfurnished that we began to run into problems with people who mistreated it. Too late, I realized that if you have never had to look after a place of your own, you could not know how to look after other people's. It wasn't an ordinary kind of excusable neglect that they left behind when they moved out (once in the middle of the night because I had dropped in to ask for their unpaid rent and they asked me to come back for it the next day), but an unhappy abusive kind that had been deliberately destructive as well as making little or no attempt to take care. I made several expensive attempts to put the house back to rights after these people left, but in the end I had to face the fact that it was hard to be an absentee landlady from so many miles away and the best thing to do was to sell it.

Meanwhile, we asked Brian and Sue to help us take some of our stuff we needed down to the island. They had been skiing at Sugar Loaf before they came up with a truck from the island and we had a great get-together before it was time for them to go. As the truck with all our belongings was pulling out of our driveway, we noticed that part of the tarpaulin was not fastened down properly. We got into the car and chased them, but Brian didn't see us and sped away. When we couldn't catch up to them in the city traffic, we gave up and went back home.

The truck had reached as far as the other side of the Champlain Bridge when a tire fell off the back and rolled into the ditch. Brian immediately pulled off to the side of the highway and rescued it. It was then that he realized that they had lost a suitcase that had also fallen out from under the loose cover, so they turned back to look for it. I can never pass over the Champlain Bridge again without laughter. The suitcase had fallen off and spilled open as they crossed the bridge the first time and, right in the middle of the river crossing, every post and rail was decorated with Sue's soiled T-shirts and underwear. "We didn't stop to pick up our laundry," Brian said. "We just left it there and drove off."

We took a lot of stuff ourselves down to the island that spring, travelling in two cars, with Tim's car breaking down as a matter of course somewhere in the wilds of Maine. Was it then or later that I had a wood stove on the seat of my little car? Tim had acquired an apartment style one over the winter, a tall slim type that was as heavy as sin, but he thought it would be useful in the hall in winter. When I stopped at the Canadian border to declare it, the customs officer looked at me as if I was mad. "Pull over and park there," he ordered impatiently. When he peered into the Datsun, he burst out laughing. "You really do have a wood stove in here!" he exclaimed. The springs of that back seat were never the same again.

Now at last the order of the day at the old house on the Thoroughfare was to do something about fixing up the interior. George Beman put up a new ceiling in the guest room that used to be Brian's room, and he helped with the kitchen ceiling and walls, too. Denise came and papered the dining room, but not before we had moved Annie's table and chairs into the kitchen and used that room as a work-room. Gail Pflaster and a friend came that summer, staying in the trailer for a week, and when other Montreal friends, David and Marika Ainley, showed up, we decided to have a dinner party. The menu was to be a real Grand Manan one, prepared by Tim, with turnip and mashed potato, and salt fish cooked with pork scraps on the electric frying pan outside. My job was to make the table as pretty as possible, with our best china and glassware and silver and a bouquet of wildflowers in the centre. We sat down happily to this elegant dinner, and I must say that our guests were all good sports as we did our communal best to ignore a great hole in the interior wall beside my lovely table, a hole that ran from ceiling to floor, exposing the black flush pipe coming down from the bathroom toilet above.

It's hard now to remember the sequence of events over that second summer, when exactly what was done. Was it that spring or the one after when my god-daughter Liz and her husband Dave came over from England, the only time I remember snow geese landing on Castalia Marsh? It had to be early May because our visitors had enjoyed the brant in the harbour, watching lines of them taking off and landing and listening to the peaceful chuckling chatter before the birds left for Arctic nesting areas later that month, so I thought these English cousins should see these other unexpected visitors and rushed them up to see nine geese that looked so different from the shining snow-white ones I remembered at Cap Tourmente. Dave muttered something disgustedly about the shabby, mud-coloured, uninteresting, feathered creatures, and we left to do what was more fun for them, which was to pick periwinkles off a lobster holding pen and bring them home to cook for supper.

I think it was later that summer when my Cat Nat friends Hugh and Mary Howson stayed in the trailer, Hugh somehow folding his long six-foot frame into the cramped space, and while they were there Tim and I rented a sander and did the floors in the living and dining room. We had had someone do the kitchen floor already and been disappointed that there was no way he could remove the scars from when the verandah had been chopped up indoors for firewood, but it was wonderful to have it shiny and clean. The other floors were amazing. When we got rid of the tar that had been all over the dining room hardwood, we found a beautiful pattern underneath. The living room floor was interesting both in its designs and in the fact that only the outside was hardwood.

The centre had been intended to be carpeted and to save money had been made out of softwood instead.

With the other inside repairs, I found I really couldn't do ceilings very well and was glad for help with that, but I discovered that I loved repairing the plaster walls. I did them in my fashion, with far from perfect but still tolerably flat results, and anyway who cared if old walls had interesting bumps? I never approved of old ladies having face lifts and trying to look like eighteen year olds because I had always loved old faces with all the lines and wrinkles that showed a lifetime of experience, so why should I even attempt to make an old house look like a new one and lose all its character? Tim was happy to leave me to get on with this kind of thing. He was starting to take more of a back seat now that the pressure was off to do urgent tasks in order to be tolerably warm and comfortable in the house, however basic our living quarters still seemed to be. He was noticeably not very well, so he saved most of his effort for the things I could not do. However, once the walls were painted white and the floors were varnished and shining, I began to feel that we could enjoy the old house at last. At least downstairs. Going upstairs, I never finished the railings because Tim couldn't stand the smell of the stripping stuff I was using, and we had much left to do with the bathroom and halls and some of the rooms upstairs.

It would take a visit from my 78-year-old Auntie Betty from England a year later for us to remove the last of the old wallpaper in the hall upstairs. Auntie Betty was amazing. She was up the stepladder before anyone could stop her, working away vigorously like she did everything. My sister once reckoned that Auntie's house in England was getting smaller all the time because every year she painted it again from top to bottom. When we sat down to eat in the old house, it was Auntie who got up in a hurry to do the dishes, practically snatching our coffee mugs out of our hands to get the job finished. We played cards with her after supper and she complained that we took too long shuffling them. "You'll shuffle the spots off them," she told us crossly. How I missed her when it was time to take her back to the airport for her trip home.

Eventually, the only old wallpaper that was left on the walls was in Darlene's room. We had been in such a hurry to have somewhere clean when we moved into the house that we had simply painted on top of it. There was one cupboard in what had been Liege's room that was left to the very last and I almost didn't repair and paint it. I sometimes wish I had done what I thought of doing, which was to put a glass frame over the back to display what the whole house had looked like when we started. It would have been a picture of dirty wallpaper and plaster coming off the walls, of tufts of horsehair and wooden laths and spiders webs and the dust of so many years.

We acquired a wood cook-stove for the kitchen that summer, a big, old, 1940s edition that took up a large corner but certainly kept the place warm. It was Tim's pride and joy to keep it stoked up, because he felt the cold so keenly, and he loved to cook on it. He didn't bake bread but he cooked roasts, turkey or any meat that was brown, anything but vegetables. He liked his food to be brown and white, a real meat and potatoes man. "Very colourful," he would say when he looked at my plate when I added lots of vegetables. He also liked to make canned salmon stew, made by meticulous cleaning of the salmon, and adding diced cooked potatoes, evaporated milk, and a large dollop of butter on top. For dessert, this was always followed by his special lemon meringue pie.

It didn't take long for Tim to teach me to like evaporated milk in my tea and coffee, a hangover from the days when that was all that was available on the island at times, and I had got to like it on Machias Seal Island, but I found it hard to punch the customary hole in the can until Bernard Larimer turned up one day with what has ever since been my favourite kitchen tool. He had made a hole in one end of a carefully whittled, smooth-rounded piece of wood and inserted a large headless nail upside down into it. I have no idea how he got it to stay so securely but all I had to do was place my 'hole-maker' on top of the can and bang it down and I had a perfect hole for pouring our evaporated milk. One 'from-away' friend later told me that she had served tea to her North Head neighbours soon after she arrived on the island and when her guests got up to leave they said, "Thank you for the tea, but we won't be coming back again unless you give it to us with Carnation Milk!"

Bernard was one of the many Grand Mananers who often dropped in for a cuppa and a chat with Tim in the kitchen. Sometimes I sat with them and listened to the stories, but if the visitor and Tim were both smoking I had to leave and go to another room as I found it hard to breathe. I learned how to play crib, but when it was chess I left them to it. I found the stories fascinating because they told of a world that was so unlike mine that they could have come from another planet. It wasn't the sea or fishing stories that had a rollicking zest to the telling, or the humorous stories told at a long slow pace until they twisted triumphantly at the end, it was the stories told offhand about what to them were ordinary dangers and difficulties from which I realized how sheltered I had been all my filtered middle-class life. It made me begin to understand how I could say something to Tim in all innocence that he would interpret as terrible in some way because of his experience with less comfortable lives. I had a lot to learn, but I was learning.

I was learning that honesty was usually better than the polite evasiveness that I was used to. Someone once said that it was the manners of the heart that really mattered and I think they were right. Tim certainly wasn't going to waste time on fake gentility. I would have to learn his truth straight, whether I liked it or not. He was always dinning into me what I should or shouldn't do now that I was living on Grand Manan, and it seemed I had never been brought up properly and hadn't the faintest idea how to behave. I smiled and talked to everyone when I should be more reserved. All this unnatural naturalist behaviour! He was horribly embarrassed if I stopped to pick flowers by the wayside or gathered 'rubbish' off the beach.

Some of his rules seemed quite sensible but I was not sure that I could agree with them all. I agreed that I would never work outside on Sunday ("But doesn't God see inside?"), or hang our underwear out on the laundry line, especially side by side, and I must always remember that it was the other person's dignity that mattered when you didn't know a person very well. It seemed my dignity didn't matter at all where Tim was concerned. If someone else did something stupid, it was because I had insisted on it being done differently and I was the silly woman from Montreal who was to blame because I didn't know any better, and he would go the length of the island saying so to save the other person's face. "But what about mine?" I protested. "Oh. yours doesn't matter," he said.

He was always saying I fussed too much about details. "My millimetre woman," he taunted me, as he sat down to have another smoke. "A millimetre here, a millimetre there, what difference does it make?" It made a huge difference to me sometimes, when I was trying to do things right fixing up the house, but of course I was not dealing with Tim's pain. It saddens me now to remember all the things that Tim did those first two summers, wracked with back and chest pain, as he struggled with windows and plumbing and the heavy containers of water, not to mention the big old fridge. My only consolation is that I think they were happy years for him as we turned his past failures into some kind of reasonable success.

Brian put up the floor of a new verandah that summer and I was in my element helping him to nail it down. It was wonderful being out there with the smell of the sea and the sound of the gulls over the harbour and it gave me happy memories of my childhood in Guyana when the bauxite camp workmen had given me a piece of wood and a hammer and nails and I had happily 'worked' beside them. I always liked being with people working with their hands, especially when they were creating something out of a pile of loose materials that came together into a positive result that could be seen and admired. He also put in a new floor in the attic after Tim had nearly come crashing down from a balancing act on the beams. Working on my own, I was proudest of all of my job of shingling the outside wall above the cellar entry that still showed where the original housing had been removed. At least I was proud until I learned that I had been misinformed. I had so carefully followed instructions to leave a space between the shingles because, they said, the shingles would expand. Of course, they didn't, and I never could look at my carefully wrong shingling without a twinge of disappointment.

We had two new additions to Tim's family that year, because Denise's Sarita arrived in the winter and Brian and Sue's Jake was born that August. Andrea came over from Germany in September and we took her to White Head to see Linwood and Lester and Beth and what was left of Tim's childhood world. We always visited the graves in the little cemetery along the road and read the names of all the family, and grieved again for the grandfather who had tragically lost both his wife and his daughter on the same day. In October, we took Andrea to the White Mountains to see the leaves, and up Mount Washington to see the view, and we took her to Montreal to stay in the Pointe Claire house after the Laws had left it, and to see John and Michèle and my mother before coming back through moose country in Maine. New England was lovely with the fall colours but so was Grand Manan when we got back, and it must have been a warm enough October because I spent a lot of time up a ladder in the last week or so while Andrea was with us, painting the outside walls.

With all the work we had put into it, the old house still looked a disgrace from the road. Peeling paint pointed to negligence and I just couldn't bear it any longer. I could only paint to a line halfway up the side of the house before feeling giddy, but I was very pleased with myself for getting that far up the ladder, especially since I used to feel giddy if I climbed as high as a mere chair. I remember feeling both very proud and very sorry for myself because all the time I worked out in the cold, Andrea and Tim were cozy inside playing cards or just talking quietly and I thought they were rotten not to come out and help, but there really was little they could do and it was good that they could have a happy time together even if I growled at them. I painted the boards very carefully, making sure every crack was filled, because we had no insulation in the walls and in winter every crack would mean a howling wind inside.

Hallowe'en came and Andrea posed for a lovely photograph, standing by the new fireplace in the living room, dressed in naval uniform and ready to go off trick-or-treating with Ryan and Dustin, before it was time for her to go back home to Germany at the beginning of November. She had no sooner gone than Christmas lights began to go up all over Grand Manan. City night lights might be wonderful year round, but for the first time I was seeing them here in December when the island goes all out to challenge the cold winter darkness.

That Christmas, with the Pointe Claire house rented to the computer men, there was no question that Tim and I would be going away to Montreal. We put up our first tree in the living room of the old house, making sure the lights could be seen from the road, and worked hard at installing something decorative and unusual outside. Remembering Michael Field's picture of the man going out in the dory to take Christmas presents to a lighthouse island, we set Tim's rowboat on the bank beside the brook. We converted our old hot water tank into a make-believe lighthouse, and I pulled out an old Santa Clause outfit that had come with all the rest of my paraphernalia. We stuffed the suit until we had a Santa who was able to stand up in the rowboat, propped up the oars, added plastic-covered boxes for presents, and stood back to admire our unique and magnificent Christmas outdoor display. We thought it was very successful. Everyone coming up the road from Seal Cove, heading straight towards us before slowing down to go round the corner and head north up-island, would be able to see our beautiful Santa delivering his presents on Christmas Day. They would see that we had brought respectability to the old house and were joining in the community celebration of the wonders of the season. We really thought we had done something special, but just how special we didn't realize until the phone rang. It was Louise Locke on the corner and she was laughing. "Look out at your Santa!" she chuckled. She laughed often that Christmas, because every time the wind blew, Santa lost his trousers.

So much for respectability. But at least we were here. We had electric heaters in every room and Tim had a roaring fire every day in the kitchen wood stove and another in the apartment stove in the hall, so we could live in the old house on the Thoroughfare in winter and not freeze ourselves to death. Tim was happy to be here and so was I, even if I missed my family. For the first time in many years, I would not hear my mother's annual Christmas lecture about the difference between Tom and Jane turkeys (I never did learn the difference) while the bird was being carved. I would not watch little Michèle open her presents or have a hug from at least one son, but I would get a warm Christmas call from them all in Montreal and from Tony and Jeannine in faraway Western Canada. I would miss my college and naturalist friends, even though Dr. Swales wrote to me faithfully and I was sent the Cat Nat newsletter that now someone else was editing, but I could send out an open invitation for everyone to "come and see the puffins!" and visit us while I enjoyed Tim's family and the new friends I was meeting on the island.

Best of all, I could look around and see what Tim and I had done to save the old house and see that we really had a home we could live in after all the hard work. We were no longer summer people, we were here to stay, and the strange prophecy that I had heard in my head on the ferry on my first visit to the island was finally being fulfilled. I might always be 'a stranger from away' but from now on I could really call Grand Manan home.

Postscript

Tim Cossaboom died of lung cancer in 1996. Before he died, he liked to joke that they had got the old house to the point that someone would come along one day and say, "I like your house. I think I'll buy it and start fixing it up."

Wendy Dathan went on to become Curator of the Grand Manan Museum and since retirement has run a little art gallery/shop in Grand Harbour. After twenty years, she is still fixing up the house that Tim said he could have liveable in three weeks.

She would like to thank all the people mentioned in her book for everything they have done to make her life special and wonderful, as well as her good friend William Edgar for his quiet patience with her computer panics, Sarah Robinson for her wonderful cover, and her marvellous publisher friend, Judy Isherwood, who makes all miracles possible.